When the People Say No

W9-AQP-961

HARPER'S MINISTERS PAPERBACK LIBRARY

When the People Say No
Conflict and the Call to Ministry

James E. Dittes

Published in San Francisco by
HARPER & ROW, PUBLISHERS
New York, Hagerstown, San Francisco, London

Unless otherwise acknowledged, biblical quotations are from *The New English Bible* © The Delegates of the Oxford University Press and The Syndics of the Cambridge University Press 1961, 1970. Reprinted by permission.

WHEN THE PEOPLE SAY NO. Copyright © 1979 by James E. Dittes. All rights reserved. Printed in the United States of America. No part of this book may be used or reproduced in any manner whatsoever without written permission except in the case of brief quotations embodied in critical articles and reviews. For information address Harper & Row, Publishers, Inc., 10 East 53rd Street, New York, NY 10022. Published simultaneously in Canada by Fitzhenry & Whiteside Limited, Toronto.

FIRST EDITION

Designed by Patricia Girvin Dunbar

Library of Congress Cataloging in Publication Data
Dittes, James E
  When the people say no.
  (Harper's ministers paperback library)
  1. Church controversies. 2. Clergy—Office.
3. Pastoral theology. I. Title.
BV652.9.D57   1979   253   77–15879
ISBN 0–06–061923–6

---

81 82 83   10 9 8 7 6 5 4 3 2

Contents

Preface

However robust is the call to ministry—the vision of need and of impact on that need in partnership with God and his people —equally robust are the disappointments on which that call sooner or later flounders. More robust still are the new visions that erupt out of those disappointments, and the sharpened focus of need together with a heightened sense of the possibility of addressing it—the new call: Durable, vital ministry, re-called out of the debris of ministry. Indeed, how could it be otherwise for ministry in the name of one whose sustained, sustaining life vaults beyond the anguish that once ended his life.

This book shares what I have learned from ministers who

have confided in me about their searing disappointments and about the new charter for ministry they have found in facing their aches. Their experiences have supplied the rich and vital case material with which this book is full, although I have changed names and circumstances to conceal personal identities. Ministers have trusted me and themselves and the resilience of their basic commitment—and God's—enough to share freely their stark moods of despair. I have listened carefully, and with wonder, to the vitality (both theirs and the Spirit's) with which despair gives shape to hope and the joy of a new call.

The first minister ever to confide in me was my grandfather, James S. Freeman. The plight he discovered at the beginning of this century is the persistent plight that still disrupts and also constitutes ministry. "The greatest problem," he said, benumbed with a weariness in his face and in his voice that registered indelibly on me as a young boy, "is how to get the people interested sufficiently in the church and what the church stands for in the community."

My grandfather kept up his skirmishes with "the people" through fifty years of faithful ministry in midwestern Presbyterian and Reformed churches, somehow sensing that those dismaying dilemmas that thwarted ministry were *part* of ministry, of that ambiguous partnership with "the people" which comprises church and ministry. His greatest problem is the greatest problem of most ministers: How can I be a minister if they will not be a church? How can I exercise my skills, sustain my commitment, do the things I am called and trained to do, if my partners will not do their part, if they keep letting me down and resisting my best ministry? Being a minister is too often like being married to someone who is not married to you. Yet this very obtuseness, when faced squarely, is fraught with vitality and with the clues to focused and effective ministry.

I think ministers will find me listening well to their experience, joined on a not unwelcome even though unfamiliar and (for books) unusual level of intimacy. Now and then I think the reader will say yes: "Yes, that's how it is; he knows! It *does* hurt that much sometimes and in that way." And I hope the reader will constantly hear me saying yes: "Yes, that tedious, discouraging work of ministry is real and important; it is where the action is—God's recreating, redemptive action."

For a book that considers the costs of ministry is an essay on the nature of the church and its ministry.

1. Ministry as Grief Work

He was despised and rejected by men;
a man of sorrows, and acquainted with grief. . . .
All we like sheep have gone astray;
we have turned everyone to his own way;
and the Lord has laid on him the iniquity of us all.
Isaiah 53:3, 6 (RSV)

To be a minister is to know the most searing grief and abandonment, daily and profoundly. To be a minister is to take as partners in solemn covenant those who are sure to renege. To be a minister is to commit, unavoidably, energy and passion, self and soul, to a people, to a vision of who they are born to be, to their readiness to share and live into that vision. To be a minister is to make that all-out, prodigal commitment to a people who cannot possibly sustain it. That is the nature of ministry, as it is of the God thus served. The minister is called by their need, by their fundamental inability to be who they are born to be, hence by their fundamental inability to share and live into that vision in which the minister invests all. To be a minister, then, as God knows, is to be forsaken, regularly and utterly, by those on whose partnership one most relies for identity, meaning, and selfhood, as these are lodged in the vocational commitment. In their forsaking ways the minister's call is rebuffed and repudiated and grieved for, over and over again; in their forsaking and in that grief the minister's call is renewed, over and over again. For the minister *is* called by their need, by their fundamental inability to live into the vision

1

and the compact into which the minister must live so totally. Ministry is called forth and occasioned by just such grief. That makes the grief no less painful and no more welcome, only to be recognized.

"How can I be a minister (which, for ministers, usually means "How can I be anybody?") if they will not be a church?" are the sorrowful and angry words of grief. But these very words of grieving for ministry are the words that constitute ministry. If they *were* a "church," if they could be the people of God, there would be no need of ministry; there could be no ministry. "I am a minister precisely because they cannot be a church" is the confession of one who recognizes ministry as grief work. The grief is never welcomed or enjoyed, certainly not sought, as though *it* constituted or certified ministry. But when the grief comes, as it does daily and decisively, it is accepted, and the grief work it occasions is welcomed as ministry. The minister, quite literally, *works through* the grief. Ministry must be in partnership; still more essentially, however, ministry is found in apartness, the apartness of people from themselves; from God; from each other; and, inevitably, from the minister and the ministry they have invited. Facing and sharing that grief, and the grief work it occasions, minister and people can discover a new and more binding kind of partnership, a partnership of apartness.

Other people may experience only a few times in a long lifetime the grief of losing a crucial life partner; the grief of a crucial promise broken by a parent (or a teacher) absolutely trusted until then; the grief of being jilted by a lover, divorced by a spouse, betrayed by a friend. In any one week a minister experiences many such moments of grief. The minister is seduced by the commitments of ministry to put near-ultimate reliance on a partnership, a mutuality, a reciprocity, or a covenant, only to discover daily and painfully that the commitment, so earnest on one side, *is* one-sided.

To be a minister is to be like a ballet dancer straining all muscles and energies into a daring leap only to find the partner not there to make the catch or steady the landing. To be a minister is to have learned one's role in a play well, to be committed to the message of the play and passionately geared for a performance, and to appear on stage to discover the rest of the cast in disarray, unprepared, or absent. To be a minister is to write an important letter, to write energetically and well, then to entrust it to careless messengers or, even worse, a careless reader.

Most other professionals hold back some selfhood to invest in family, hobbies, luncheon clubs, days off, or even church. A minister is all-out a minister, and usually nothing but a minister, twenty-four hours a day. So when ministry is thwarted and the minister feels not a minister, there is the emptiness and grief of being nobody. Most other professionals find their "clients" dependent on them; clients follow the rules and roles set by the lawyer, nurse, auto mechanic, or physician. But ministers are in a partnership. Their work depends on invitation and response from others. Lawyers and physicians and nurses and auto mechanics take charge. Ministers plant seeds.

Moreover, ministers plant seeds—on purpose, as part of their ministry—on rocky soil, where the seeds are mostly doomed. Where the soil is good and the climate is nourishing, there is no need for ministry; plants seed themselves naturally and grow abundantly. Some ministers do seek haven from grief, and hence from ministry, where faith and community, perhaps even love and justice, do seem to be thriving abundantly. But the ministry of the God who has ever pursued an apostate people precisely in their faithlessness and brokenness is called to flourish exactly where it can never flourish, in those corners of life where it is most needed and hence most unwelcome. When the minister hears a comfortable affirmation and acceptance, there may be cause for self-scrutiny. Ministry may still lie ahead. When the people say no, ministry may have been reached. Ships are meant to travel through the waves of the high seas; if the surface is always placid, they must still be in the harbor.

"Acquainted with Grief . . ."

To grieve is to take two coffee cups from the cupboard in the morning, only to remember that one's wife is dead or separated . . . and to have to put one cup back.

To grieve is to start joyfully into the gift shop, one's eye attracted by the perfect gift in the window, only to remember that the child is dead . . . and to walk on down the street, heavily.

To grieve is to start out from the office with habitual joy at the end of the day, toward the usual rendezvous with one's lover, only to remember the long, anguished phone call of the night before . . . and to go home alone.

To grieve is to be delighted with the snapshot prints at the drugstore counter and impulsively to order duplicates to share with one's mother, only to remember that she died six months previously . . . and to say to the clerk, "Never mind."

To grieve is to have an especially interesting job come into the shop, a job one automatically routes to a favorite young protege, only to have the word come back that he has just quit and gone to work for a competitor . . . and to look up, confused, saying, "Who can do this?"

To grieve is to wake up on a brilliant sunny morning with spontaneous, unbidden anticipation of playing golf, only to be reminded instantly by heavy limbs that one has had a stroke . . . and to close one's eyes, now moist.

To grieve is to invest prime energy and love into a sermon for a much loved people, only to be reminded that it was not heard: "I enjoyed your sermon." "That was a cute illustration." "Wasn't the choir lovely this morning?"

To grieve is to pour one's energies for months and years into the struggles of a beleagured minority group or a beleagured marriage or a beleagured teenager—standing by patiently and wisely and lovingly, and indeed making a crucial difference—only to have the group or couple or teenager, having found themselves, shun you as a threatening enemy.

To grieve is to introduce into a discussion at the deacons' meeting some biblical allusions, such as some of the ringing phrases from Romans 8, as one has spent years training oneself to do and supposes to be standard in a Christian community, only to have the deacons look blank and someone remark, "You ministers sometimes do pick up some funny language."

To grieve is to presuppose among one's people a Christian concern for the oppressed and to build upon this foundation an alertness to the problem of civil rights for homosexuals or Puerto Ricans, only to have this foundation manifestly absent: "Stick to religion and to our own kind of people."

To grieve is to commit oneself seriously to the pulpit committee's assurance that the people of the church want to develop intentional small groups, such as house churches and prayer cells, only to discover the utmost resistance: "Well, folks are pretty busy here in the evenings; Sunday morning is about all we can manage."

To grieve is to accept the pulpit committee's assurance that the people would not be prejudiced against a woman as minister and that she could function effectively, only to be confronted by a barrage of offensive putdowns.

To grieve is to have one's earnest readiness to share the depths of the people's lives frustrated repeatedly by their attempt to assign one to superficial roles: "Just give the invocation at the women's luncheon; please try to get around to each of our homes at least once a year, even though you can't stay long."

To grieve is to prepare earnestly for the training session that the church school teachers asked for, only to have them spend the entire evening preoccupied with discipline problems for the individual students, problems about getting supplies in and out of the supply closet, and questions of scheduling the year-end picnic.

To grieve is to invest years of heady anticipation and hearty preparation in taking one's place as the minister among the people of God, only to discover the visions of that anticipation and the fruits of that preparation disparaged and frustrated by those very people. The visions have been bolstered by so much: by the study of church history, disclosing the high unassailed and unambiguous status of clergy in the established churches of the past; by memories of one's childhood and adolescence when total loving support seemed to close around the minister or oneself as the "pre-theolog"; by the offhand abstract language of much transcendental theology so deliberately out of touch with the realities of the institutional church as to speak easily and glibly of the committed people of God, or the functioning body of Christ as though it were fact; by most teaching of pastoral theology, which instructs a minister how to take a part in the script by assuming all the others are playing their parts; by one's own lifelong yearnings for a closely supporting community; by the rhetoric of ordination sermons.

The vision is also sustained by the very impediments in the preparation for ministry. Sterile seminars in Bible and theology, if endured, seem justified by that vision of the community soon to be entered in which Bible and theology are validated and learned by being lived. The belittling tendered the apprentice theological student by a training church enhances the vision of the time one will assume a full and respected place as *the* minister.

Through theological training and into first assignments one can endure many years of anguish and ambiguity by keeping this vision lofty. One can be sustained and guided through an entire ministry by the vision, so long as it is kept apart and beyond, never located, never confused with a particular people or place or program. Knowing full well that no community, no parish, no people can embody the vision—through such grief work, anticipating the death of the vision by knowing it cannot fully live, the minister stays in ministry.

To locate the vision, to ground it in a place and people, to try to lodge it in a program or parish who cannot but dislodge it, sooner or later—that is to invite grief without preparing for it. When the vision is identified with a particular assignment or community—one's first full-time church, one's first church as the senior minister, those people in the inner city who are committed and free of the shackles of the institutional church, or the church in the university town where people are literate about Bible and theology—or with particular people—the counselee with whom one has developed such close rapport through long intimate hours, the one family who seems on the same wavelength with each other and with you, the no-nonsense group of businessmen working with you on the public housing project—such grounding of vision sets one up for grief. For no people, no person can ever become that fully responsible, fully responsive partner to ministry envisioned by theological abstraction, personal yearning, or historical simplification. Yet ministry nevertheless seems to require and propel that intensity of investment, that dancer's leap, that actor's total immersion into a role that presupposes just such unswerving partners, equally invested and totally committed.

Swallowing Grief

He was oppressed, and he was afflicted,
  yet he opened not his mouth;
like a lamb that is led to the slaughter,
  and like a sheep that before its shearers is dumb,
  so he opened not his mouth.

Isaiah 53:7 (RSV)

There are two ways to swallow grief dumbly, both ways making it more poisonous than nutritious. One can deny the life that was lived, the partnership that was shared. Or one can deny the death, the real limits and breakdown of the partnership. The widower can throw away the now-offending second coffee cup and the jilted lover can burn the letters, as though the life and love had never been lived and shared. Death is triumphant. Or the widower can continue to make the second cup of coffee, keep all of his wife's clothes and room as they were, and the lover can continue to haunt the rendezvous and reread the letters as though they were fresh, just as though nothing had changed, just as though the partnership persisted, undaunted. Death is denied.

The minister can swallow grief either way: death triumphant or death denied. The minister can repudiate the visions, deny the tremendous and total investment made in them, exaggerate the abandonment by partners, see only the assault on the vision not the visions. That is, the minister can flee the ministry, either by actually resigning from the church payroll or by becoming resigned to a visionless, partnerless occupation, by becoming jaded and "professional," mechanically going through the motions, like a zombie actor reciting long memorized lines on a darkened and empty stage to an empty house. This is the path some take, stockading themselves, darkening the house, with drink, with golf, with cynical banter with fellow

professionals. These are the ministers that novelist John Up-
dike knows and portrays so well. They have protected their
visions by abandoning them and by no longer caring whether
they have partners or effect. They go through the motions.
The motions may be those of worship or preaching or counseling or municipal politics or jovial backslapping or studying or
more efficient administrative operations or personal spiritual-
ity. But, like the jilted lover who protects himself from further
grief by staying home evenings and reading romantic stories,
such ministry-like motions are totally self-contained and get
nowhere. The minister, purposely defensive, heeds not the
needs or reactions of prospective partners. The minister hears
only the no.

Or the minister may cling tenaciously to the vision and expectation of partnership and deny its limits, which are clearly
evident in the practice of ministry. The minister pretends not
to hear the no. The minister may find or seek out those few
—celebrated as "the faithful remnant"—who seem to offer the
maximum possibility of partnership, and concentrate ministry
on them, who least need it. Or the minister may find a few
selective avenues of ministry that seem to generate a response
—counseling often seems to make people warm and responsive, political action puts one in touch with those who know
how to stroke back. And effective ministry will be stockaded as
safely as possible, like the jilted lover closeted and reading old
love letters.

The death-defying minister's intense addiction to a few
forms may not be much different from the jaded minister's
casualness about going through the motions. Both protect
themselves from facing the grief of disappointment in partnership, past and future, by effectively shielding themselves with
the motions of ministry from the majority of those to whom
they would minister but from whom they feel separated by the
risk of broken covenant.

There is a common way of denying the seriousness of the no, of clinging to the expectations of partnership and denying the radical violation of the partnership that does in fact exist. This is to suppose that the people's "delinquencies" need just a bit more coaching and training to remedy. The people's failing in partnership is not taken *seriously;* it is seen as only a temporary and technical defect. They can be taught the scripts for playing the people of God. They can be taught from the pulpit or from the Bible or from the denominational manuals; from the longings of the minister's heart and from the abstractions of theology. Having been taught the script, they will, it is assumed, readily play the part. Let the people be scolded or instructed or cajoled into proper partnership. The minister's vision is grounded just on the other side of this locker room pep talk: In the second half of this ministry, the team will be functioning smoothly.

Another way of trivializing the failure of partnership takes the form of the periodic sociological exposé, in which discrepancies between the people's notions of church and ministry and the minister's notions are paraded, as though this conflict were a unique and exceptional and catastrophic event rather than part of every minister's experience and a basic necessity for constructive ministry. The sociological exhibition, like back-fence gossip, attempts to preserve the norm (in this case, of partnership) as the rule and to isolate the contradiction as a unique exception.

Or the minister may simply swallow the grief quite literally, keep it private, personal, and ignored. He or she will go relentlessly on, oblivious to the disappointments of failed partnership, heedless of the dance leaps taken and uncaught, the supporting cast in disarray. This is an heroic posture of ministry and perhaps a necessary one. But it, like the other responses, swallows the grief, refuses to take seriously the visions and their frustration, and so fails to learn from the grief and to find ministry *in* the grief.

Working through Grief

Yet it was the will of the Lord to bruise him;
  he has put him to grief . . .
the will of the Lord shall prosper in his hand;
  he shall see the fruit of the travail of his soul and be satisfied;
by his knowledge shall the righteous one, my servant,
  make many to be accounted righteous.

Isaiah 53:10–11 (RSV)

It is the extraordinary claim of Christian and Jewish faith that God works through grief. Contradicting all natural expectations (and especially the American prizing) of the efficacy of smoothness and success, the Bible and the believer perceive God fashioning and disclosing, in the midst of brokenness and desolation of spirit—indeed out of the very raw materials of brokenness and desolation—a wholeness more substantial and a life more vital than can be found otherwise. From creation out of chaos to the promise of salvation in the midst of apocalypse, the Bible records the works of a God who fashioned a people out of slaves, wanderers, and exiles; intimate and lasting covenant out of the most faithlessly broken covenant; dramatic life out of the most forsaken death; a community of faith out of those in most fearful disarray.

The record of the Old Testament is nothing if not the record of a God who experiences the constant grief of the abandonment of his people and who enters into that abandonment and lives into that grief to unlock the creative energies within it. It is only after Adam and Eve have violated their first covenant and are hiding in fear and shame that God seeks them out, first appears to them face to face and sets in motion a drama of salvation that takes with utmost seriousness the persisting bond between God and people and with equal seriousness the ruptures to that bond. It is in the squalid faithlessness of the Jewish people, time after time after time abandoning their part of the partnership with God, that God is most powerfully present, scourging the rupture to the bond with fierce wrath, tenderly nurturing the remnant of bond that is within the very experience of grief. Indeed, the Lord of the Old Testament knows precisely what it is to "see the fruit of the travail of his soul and be satisfied."

The record of the New Testament is nothing if not precisely the story of ministry in the midst of broken expectations as in no other place; indeed, the story of a message and a ministry conveyed *by means of* broken expectations. Incarnate deity in a village stable confounded the wisest expectations of the wise men. (But by taking seriously both the commitment in those expectations and their radical destruction, they learned a lesson.) Jesus' ministry consistently frustrated the highest religious expectations of the Jewish people as recorded in their law and guarded by the lawkeepers. Jesus' ministry with his disciples was one disappointment after another, as each repeatedly frustrated the expectations of the other. Jesus would not dispute and teach as a good rabbi should but rather indirectly, in parables and in deeds. The cheering Palm Sunday crowd abandoned him, as he abandoned their expectations. He celebrated communion in the midst of betrayal and finally lived out salvation in the most forlorn of deaths. The teaching and the work of Christ proceeded precisely by means of breaking expectations. Jesus caused grief and Jesus suffered grief; the grief was necessary for the uncovering of wholeness. If people had persisted in living only in their expectations, they would have kept themselves separated from God—the fate of the Pharisees; so, too, with those who abandoned their expectations, once frustrated, such as the rich young ruler. Wise men, disciples, women, finally Jesus himself, in the agony of Gethsemane and Golgotha, persisted in living *in* their grief and abandonment and wresting from it new vision, new commitment, new guidance, and new personhood. It is the *intent* of the Lord to reach people in grief, his and theirs, as perhaps they can be reached in no other way. "It was the will of the Lord to bruise him; he has put him to grief. . . ."

The creative healing power of grief is dramatically confirmed in human experience—so long as one is dealing with real grief, which denies neither the dreams nor their dashing, denies neither the commitment nor its betrayal, denies neither the expectations nor their frustration, denies neither life nor death—so long as one takes seriously, in the grief, the earnestness of the vision and the earnestness of its shattering.

Lovers disappoint each other bitterly, yet, holding fast to the radical commitment that has made them so vulnerable to the disappointments and taking equally seriously the severity of the disappointment and the grief, they enfold each other and find in their mingled tears and despair an intimacy and a trust and a hope far greater than that which they found dashed.

The new widower takes down two coffee cups and then sadly puts one back; there is both a shared life to be celebrated and a death to be recognized; in the grief he ponders in such moments, in that quick review of his life with, and now without, his wife, he comes to enhanced and deepened appreciation of the relationship and of himself in separation from her. He is more a whole person and readier to enter new relationships for having lived through such moments of grief.

The young woman is in despair as she recovers from her hysterectomy. She does not deny the loss and the grief by clinging blindly to the now-impossible dream of having children, nor does she deny the grief by repudiating that vision with a callous shrug. Instead, she lives into that grief by living into the vision and into its defeat until she discovers deeper aspirations and fulfillments. The personal fulfillment, indeed the experience of motherhood, is not to be denied even though giving birth is to be denied. Her spirit is opened to new vocational possibilities, new forms of motherhood, once she faces fully her grief and sees in it two things: the deep aspirations that were lodged in her hopes for children and frustrated by the hysterectomy; and the absoluteness of that frustration, the complete death of her hopes for children of her own. Facing her grief means facing the depth of her hopes and the depths of her despair; facing her grief becomes the means of finding new expression for those hopes.

This book suggests that the call to the ministry functions in the same way. There is a call to the covenants of ministry, then constant frustration of the expectation built into that call, then formidable and powerful re-call to ministry in the grief of those frustrations. This seems not unlike the redemptive processes displayed in the Bible and the intentions of God for his servant as recorded in Isaiah: "Yet it was the will of the Lord to bruise him; he has put him to grief . . . the will of the Lord shall prosper in his hands; he shall see the fruit of the travail of his soul and be satisfied." The minister is called into a ministry of grief, is re-called to deepen and reform and refresh and redirect that ministry by, quite literally, working through the grief that befalls every venture into ministry. This book looks especially at the grief of failed partnerships, the grief experienced by the minister in the abandonment of those to whom ministry is directed and with whom it is to be shared. "How can I be a minister when they will not be a church?" This book suggests how.

The minister is called to particular partnerships, to particular roles that require others to play corresponding and reciprocal roles. Indeed, ministry of the living God who works *in* history and by incarnation does not exist if it is not lodged or placed in particular callings, in specific covenants and partnerships with particular people at particular times and places. The call to ministry often comes precisely in such callings, personal needs to be met, organizational rhythms and systems with a place to be filled, traditions to be lived out. Yet such callings, in particular times and places by particular people, can never make good the call they make. This book is about the disappointments and abandonments—inevitable and healthy—with which ministers' partners must eventually respond to ministry. These abandonments, if the grief is lived into, themselves become new callings. (We must not deny the abandonment and frustration that ministers supply their partners. Ministers, too, let down the partnership. The book does not deny this, but it is not about it. Enough other books scold ministers for their delinquencies. This book attempts to support them in their distress and to redirect the energies of despair.)

Preaching, teaching, counseling, enabling deacons, arranging committees, leading prayer, pricking consciences, organizing picketing or petitions—all respond to a bid, a calling by another person, a need or readiness expressed implicitly or explicitly, and presuppose a response in partnership. The minister moves and expects a reciprocal move by the people. Sometimes that happens; the dancers are in step, the ecological system is in balance. Frequently it does not happen; the dancers are out of step, a disruptive mutation dislodges the partnership out of its ecological niche. The people fail to make the complementary move. (The people say no, the people fail to say thank you, the people get distracted and preoccupied with organizational machinery.) Or the people make another move, an unexpected move, which seems to call from the minister a move that contradicts ministry. (The people say pray, the people say heal, the people say perform, the people say sacrifice.) The momentum of ministry is stopped, the call contradicted, the partnership betrayed. There is reason for all of the grief the minister feels and more. What is necessary is that the minister experience the grief fully, live fully in it, work fully through it; repudiate neither the authenticity and loftiness of the call to which ministry was responding, the importance of the partnership that was expected, nor deny the genuineness and fullness and authenticity of the betrayal, the frustration. The people *did* say no after they said yes and after the minister was lured by the yes. Fully viewed, taking both the yes and the no absolutely seriously, the grief transforms the partnership and recalls to ministry; it does not end the partnership or ministry.

Taking the Yes Seriously

The people meant their calling and whatever the calling meant to them. From their perspective, their present no is in continuity with the earlier yes. Jesus said he came to fulfill the Law not to repudiate it, even as he systematically frustrated all those expectations of people based on the Law. The Law affirmed something Jesus wanted to affirm, pointed to something Jesus wanted to point to. If one can believe the yes and not fear to look for it in the no, one will find it. The no is a word *in* the conversation and has a meaning in the conversation. It does not end the conversation.

If the people say, "We enjoyed your sermon," perhaps they do not mean to slight it or to put it aside; perhaps that is only their way—their only way—of talking about it. Perhaps they mean simply: "We were touched or moved or pricked by the sermon, too much so to verbalize it comfortably; so we both express and disguise this reaction with 'enjoyed your sermon.'" Perhaps they mean: "We admire your learning and wisdom, your knowledge of the Bible and your ability to make it speak to us, so much that we are intimidated and do not know how to enter into your league." Perhaps they mean: "You made us angry, but we never felt permission to be angry in church." And perhaps the response means just what the minister likely feels it means: a stuporous, bland, heedless, perhaps even inattentive, reception. But what does *this* mean

among the churchgoers? Why do people persistently come to
church and persistently hear not? This is still part of some
awestruck wonder at the Word. If people do feel themselves
unworthy or unneedy, if the spoken Word is too lofty or too
mean or too mysterious and arcane, why do they come? Or if
they come, why do they persistently turn off? There is *some*
dialogue going on. The people *are* responding, if the minister
has ears to hear. Just as the first invitation to preach the sermon or their attendance at the worship service are a placing
of their lives into some kind of relationship with the Word as
preached, so is their response at the end of the sermon.
Though their response may not be what the minister expected
in the partnership, the minister would do well to assume that
the people are still in the partnership. Their response transforms the covenant and the call by extending it.

If the minister listens to the no for what it means strictly in
the short run to him or her, the minister, then there is heard
only the denial of expectations. But the minister can—or so
this book asserts—listen to the response for what it means to
the people and hence to the minister and ministry in the long
run.

There is a literalistic reading of people that is sometimes
practised even by ministers who have become quite sophisticated about reading the Bible without literalistic shackles.
Such literalism skims off, at face value, the superficial level of
people's response. Because the minister reads glibly, he or she
easily assumes that the people are being glib, that the no
means only what it quite literally seems to mean at first hearing. The more sophisticated minister reads the words of the
Bible in the context in which they were written and asks what
they meant to the writer before asking what they may mean to
the reader. What spoken or unspoken implications, what cul-
tural or individualized connotations of the language are there
for the speaker? In that particular context, what impact, larger

than any literal reading of the words, did the speaker or writer mean to communicate? Why not accord contemporary church people the same sophistication of intention, either conscious or unconscious, and learn to read their words for what they mean to *them* in *their* context?

Taking the No Seriously

Much as the people's response is part of the continuing partnership, it *is* a rebuff to the minister's move, and intended to be so. The minister has responded to the call, but apparently not quite on target. The minister has entered into the compact, but with too compacted a ministry, has fit into too narrow an ecological niche. The people seem to be saying, "We feel you but not exactly where we hurt or yearn; we are not there." The minister's role is going to have to be transformed.

This asks for a sacrifice by the minister. Not the simple sacrifice of high salary or high social status; those things are given up relatively easily. The sacrifice is being willing to lose one's identity, to be swallowed up into chaos. For the minister does make the moves of sermon or any other role of ministry with an energy and an investment and an ultimacy in which they provide identity and important meaning to the minister. This is why the minister is so ready to hear the resistive response as an attack; there is much of importance here to be defensive about. The minister is asked to respond to the experience of taking a flying leap and finding no one there to steady the landing by taking another flying leap in a different direction in a style for which there has been no practice nor script and to a place where again there may be no partner.

Remember that the people's words do *not* provide close literal guidance for the new calling. They are only saying: "We are not just where you are aiming." To take literally their call to pray or heal or anything else is surely to enter into a new blind alley. One needs to probe beneath the surface of their calling to find the new call within it. Sometimes this probing can be done verbally, until the minister does feel some assurance about the new target and the new response, hears the new call. But sometimes a minister has to probe behaviorally, not verbally, beneath the resistive response that is a re-calling. The minister has to take the leap, has to venture a new response and see where it gets.

Indeed, most ministry is probably in this chaotic, interim mode. Seldom in stable balance, the ecology is more often in a state of disruption, which means it is always evolving. Most of us live by the light-at-the-end-of-the-tunnel myth that points to a time when all *will* be stable, and one can settle down to ministry with partners responding as expected. In fact, a yes response, an apparently stable partnership, may be the most resistive and denying of all; it may well represent a sophisticated encapsulation of the minister by really shackling ministry, keeping it in a box, keeping it from reaching out effectively into disruption.

Ministry is not in answering questions or in having questions answered. Ministry is precisely in the creative process of continually reshaping questions and reshaping answers. Ministry is in the process of re-calling, reforming, revisioning, ever peeling off what is partial and encrusted in human resignation and contentment with forms so as to leave room for the boiling vitality of God's creative, redemptive spirit.

2. Through Inarticulate Groans: Especially the Groans That Sound Like No

In the same way the Spirit comes to the aid of our weakness. We do not even know how we ought to pray, but through our inarticulate groans the Spirit himself is pleading for us, and God who searches our inmost being knows what the Spirit means, because he pleads for God's people in God's own way.

Romans 8:26–27

This way of the Spirit—coming to the aid of our weakness by dwelling in it and making our groans its own—is not the common way of ministers. Ministers more often respond to our inarticulate groans by comforting us or else by teaching us to groan more articulately. If we do not know how to pray, ministers will tell us that and will teach us how we ought to pray. Such comfort, such remedy is all *ad*-ministered—ministered *to*—from a posture outside the groans. The way that enters *within* the misspokenness and unspeakableness of our despair, the way of pleading and searching *through* our inarticulate groans, is not a popular way of ministry; people want their groans comforted or articulated. Nor, certainly, is it a "professional" way of ministry; it treacherously risks professional identity and threatens to swallow vocation. It is the way of the Spirit, "God's own way."

The groans that are totally and rawly inarticulate are the easiest to minister within—the stammering or voiceless mouthings of the stroke victim; the sobs of the widow; the raw rage of teenager, black, or others socially disinherited; the joyful or pained babbling of the infant; the embarrassed giggling in the co-ed preconfirmation class; the gasps issuing from a failing heart, failing marriage, failing career, or other faded vision. To be sure, such groans *may* be so fearful that ministers escape them by transforming the groans into articulations that *can*, quite literally, be handled: supplying words to the victims of stroke or of society, hurrying their groaning along to a conclusion; *adult*erating the infant's babbling; converting the widow's mantra of despair, "No, no, no," or the failure's explosive "Why?" into propositional language so they can be answered with a ready yes or because; interpreting the undercurrent of embarrassment as disorder to be quelled.

But more often, ministers can enter the groans as groans and share the pleading within: simply hold the trembling hand and tremble a bit, stuttering and silent, too; or give voice to the groan *as groan:* "What a frustration!" "There's just no answer in sight, is there?" "How could they do this to you!" "Pray? No way; no words come." ". . . He pleads for God's people in God's own way."* The minister enters the groans

---

*Some groans are not inarticulate at all but are unambiguously articulate —the hunger pangs of the starving, the "Help!" of the drowning victim or the victim of injustice. Such cries as these translate, in the same breath, into demands for action. To offer food or a helping hand in these cases is to respond directly to the articulated cries not to impose "help" prematurely and artificially out of the need of the "helper" to suppress the groans or inarticulateness. Such response is not limited to *ministry,* since such help is what any human being does for another. Some of the less articulated and more persisting overtones of these groans would seem to be occasions for ministry: the groans of the indignity that accompanies the hunger and injustice, the groans of guilt of the bystanders who turned aside, the groans of guilt over surviving when others didn't, the groans of despair over preventing repetition. These are the groans that invite that special ministry of the spirit, the ministry that can enter into the groaning, a sharing that helps its rhythms to resolve, at their own pace, into articulation.

until they, following their own natural rhythm, and the Spirit's, abate ("no, no, no" and "why" become "let it be") or become articulate (rage focuses on a target and remedy). But the minister does not enter *in order* to yield abatement or articulation. Ministry is in the groaning not in its abatement or its articulation. Because the minister does not need the abatement or articulation in order to claim ministry, he or she does not need to impose resolution. Ministry can let the groaning and the Spirit move to resolution at its own pace and on its own terms, liberated and nourished to do so in part by the minister's sacrificial presence in the groaning.

Imposing Facile Form on the Groans

Even when the inarticulate groans are allowed to be inarticulate, and thus left open to the Spirit, some other groans may *seem* articulate, and thus tempt close handling. These are the groans that seem to articulate, with the minister's own groans, a quest of ministry. These tempt the minister to respond more to that apparent articulation than to the groans. The groans can be made into questions or requests that the minister feels ready, even impatient, to answer. "I wish you could get my kids interested in church"—the question triggers the minister's own ready yearning; of course he or she will try to "interest" the kids in the church program. But that is to be heedless of what the question means to the parent—perhaps the parent's misgivings about the kids' distance from the church; perhaps a guarding of the parents' own distance from church and minister, protected here by distracting attention to the kids; perhaps anxieties about the kids' distance from the parents.

"Why did God do that to me?" The groan of despair is there. If entered and searched, the groan can unfold to the pleadings of guilt or of anger over an unrequited covenant with God (and possibly others) or of a sense of having been seduced into faith and abandoned or of primitive infantile raw loneliness. However, instead of listening for what these groans mean to the groaner, the minister can easily hear the sounds for what they mean to him or her—perhaps a challenge to faith, perhaps an invitation for theological explanation, perhaps a trigger for facile thumbing of the Bible for proof texts, perhaps a lead into a bid to attend church and adult Bible study or to join the group of widows the minister has begun to organize.

"Pray for me, give me money, counsel me, sign my petition, call on me, preach Christ to me, complain to City Hall for me, baptize my baby, explain the Bible to me. . . ." Such requests readily trigger a set of responses the minister is motivated and practiced to deliver; praying, giving, counseling, and all the other requested activities assume forms articulated out of ministers' own needs and history. The forms are not shaped out of the groans. It is not responsive ministry but repertory ministry. Whatever groans pour into the abyss, the same fixed echo answers back. The groaner, not knowing how to pray or how to ask for ministry, gets dial-a-prayer's recorded message.

Some groans may look like invitations for familiar ways and thus distract the minister from the Spirit's way—pleading for God's people *through* their groans, inarticulate or of seeming articulation. Groans that easily sound like yes or even please to the minister—especially a minister used to hearing no from the people and from within—are hard to hear as groans and to enter into for what they mean to the groaners.

Hearing the Groans as Demands to Defy

Still more difficult to minister *through* are the groans that seem to *dis*articulate the minister's expectations. These groans can sound like questions or demands that the minister feels necessary to repudiate; they sound like must: "Pray for me, give me money, counsel me, sign my petition. . . ." Such requests may well seem to demand particular forms of ministry that have been intentionally excluded from a minister's repertory. If these groans are articulated by the minister's hearing into shapes that he or she now regards as hollow forms, as distractions from ministry, or as false ministry, then the minister has to deal with them accordingly, by rejecting the request as articulated. The groaning itself, and whatever need and definition of ministry may lie within it, is overlooked as surely when the request is rejected or corrected as when it is answered. In either case the groans are interpreted to match contours meaningful to the minister not explored to discover the pleading within them that may be meaningful to the groaner and to the Spirit. It is still repertory ministry. It is like Professor Henry Higgins fashioning a woman to his liking and comfort, transforming Eliza Doolittle's moaning sounds into articulated Oxonian English and thereby making her unfit to be a flower girl or much of anything else but the professor's consort and handmaiden.

"Call in every home every year" may say the Bishop, the pulpit committee, the deacons, the innuendoes in the narthex. To the minister this expectation may represent an assignment unwelcome and objectionable on any number of legitimate personal and professional grounds. It makes the minister a busy puppet or a constantly casual guest; it defines a superficial mechanical ministry, generating statistics and indifference to serious matters; it contradicts the deeper ministry that is found in more intensive moments of crisis counseling, collaboration on political action, or concerted Bible study; it challenges the minister's authority and status as a professional (salesmen for aluminum siding call in homes on an annual quota, not doctors and others with important professional services to render). Because the expectations mean such things to the minister, they must be defied, the expecters reeducated, and the expectations reshaped to match the minister's repertory.

But what if one asks what these expectations may mean to the people? What if they are indeed groans that only seem articulate to a minister's limited hearing, selectively tuned by his or her own groaning needs to define and claim and defend ministry? Our despair and loneliness may be so profound, longings for our life and home to be touched by the holy and the meaningful may be so primitive and so elusive, so far from access or answer, that we know how to give them no better expression than such patter—"The minister should call" or "I won't give up my place on the Altar Guild" or "We need you to give the invocation at our Thursday women's luncheon" or "I try to sit quietly during the organ prelude, but there is so much to say to people." The very inanity of the request, which is what annoys when it is taken at face value, is or could be the principal clue that this *is* essentially inarticulate groaning. Of course such patter, like the hurried "paternoster" that gives us that word, is not praying properly. The minister wishes people could pray properly, both for their sake and because he or she would feel more securely a minister if they did. But to teach them how to pray properly is to suppress the prayer in the groaning, which has in it as much urgent, cowed yearning as the persistent mumbling of the paternoster. The way of the Spirit is to enter this groaning and plead with it—and it is part of the way of the Spirit not even to worry about whether this qualifies to be called ministry. The way of the Spirit finds means to recognize and share the dim remembrance of promises, the flickering trust in those promises, and the repressed yearnings for their enactment.

When the Spirited minister hears "Call in my home regularly," he or she doesn't haggle over definitions of ministry but is ready to read and preach of Jacob's lonely wrestling, of

Moses' final vigil, of the agonies of Job and David, of the exiled Jews and the rejected Jesus. The Spirited minister is ready to listen to the groaner's story of how promises of power and meaning were once heard and trusted in childhood, in early career, in marriage vows, in church life, in the social conscience of adolescence; and how these have dwindled to the fatuous chatter of coffee breaks, television, PTA telephoning, and narthex pleasantries. The Spirited minister is ready to hear and to speak about how transcendent visions have receded and how they have been replaced by more manageable charms and idols, such as Regular Calls by the Minister.

Such ministry as this, it usually turns out, is followed by fruits—people more alert to and energetic about those dimensions of worship and caring, mission and service for which the minister aspired, even groaned, on their behalf. But these outcomes, liberated by ministry, can never be designated and engineered as the minister's objectives; that would be new repertory, new *ad*-ministry. These outcomes must be energized by the people's groanings not engineered by the minister's.

Hearing the Groan as No and the No as Groan

It is so hard to hear the groans as groans. It may be harder for clergy than for anyone else to let the groans be groans, to enter into them as they are, to let their rhythms and energies find their own course, to minister *through* the groans not *to* them, to pray in the very language *of* the groans not in other language *about* them.

Clergy have difficulty hearing meaning and call in the inarticulate, because they are trained and committed, even addicted, to rely on the articulate, the words and symbols that speak lucidly about and to experience. So clergy are tempted to transform raw inarticulate groanings into measurable and answerable articulated complaints; they readily respond to the articulated guise and ignore the disguised inarticulate.

Clergy have difficulty hearing meaning and call in groans, because they are accustomed, commissioned, even addicted, to put an end to groaning. So they tend to cut short the groaning and to attend to its resolution; this may mean imposing solutions of their own invention, adopting the solutions suggested by the groaners (which is different from letting the groaning find its own solution), or contending against the solutions suggested by the groaners. It also may mean, as this section discusses, defending their own solutions against the opposition of the groaners.

Clergy have difficulty finding meaning and call arising out of the experience of others—*"God's own people"*—because they are accustomed by the expectations of professors, church members, and their own inner yearnings, to locate initiative and responsibility for ministry in themselves. So they tend to feel naked and guilty—not "ministers"—if they are not articulating clearly, ending groans, and doing so with demonstrable initiative, energy, and effect.

Articulation, healing, and initiative are not flaws of ministry; they are necessary elements of ministry. They are also the elements of ministry that make it difficult to minister, Spirited, through inarticulate groans. If it is difficult to enter into the raw inarticulate groans, into the groans that seem to ask for responses the minister may be too ready to offer, into groans that seem to ask for responses the minister may be too ready to deny, how much more difficult it is to enter into the groans that seem to be rejecting what the minister may be too ready to offer. The groans, the voices, that seem to say no to the minister's yes are especially devastating when the no is being said to a yes that minister and people once shared. It seems to the minister that they are saying no to their own yes, a yes on which minister has relied and on which ministry has been built. These are harder to hear as groans, as calls to constructive ministry, because the seeming articulations are so easy to take personally and as destructive of ministry.

"Don't. . . . I won't. . . . Don't pray that way, don't ask me to pray at all. . . . I won't sign any petitions. . . . Don't ask me to give up my ever-rising standard of living. . . . I won't accept spiritual or moral disciplines. . . . Don't suck me into your institutional programs. . . . Don't expect me to take the sermons, or the counseling, or the Bible study as seriously as you do. . . . I won't acknowledge authority of minister or ministry over my life, even after it may have worked some miracles, and maybe not even any place in my life. . . . Don't expect me to stay with a project or a committee or a conviction sufficiently to match your own enthusiasms or the needs that aroused my early interest. . . ."

No *is* a groan, and a highly inarticulate groan. It signals distress but does not define or locate it. It tells only that a person needs to stay away from something or everything, needs to build some shield or space around a self that must somehow feel fragile or fragmented. No is hardly more articulate than ouch and often means much the same thing: Something (or perhaps everything) hurts or threatens, and I must reflexively back away. No, like ouch, usually signals pain and fear. It is a genuine groan. It is also so inarticulate, so lacking in clues as to *what* is painful or feared, that the only way to minister to it is through it. The minister enters into the experience of the groaning no, sharing it as partner, rather than fighting it as the adversary into which it is tempting to be cast. The minister tries to feel what it is like to be this person coming close but turning away from Bible study, turning aside the petition to City Hall.

No to Bible Study

What is it about the mystery, the authority, the expectations, the invitations, the promises, the stories, or the people
of the Bible that is disrupting? What clues or calls to ministry
are there in a no to Bible study? One minister who tried to
share just such groaning by a thirty-year-old mother found
out. What distress was signalled by her no to Bible study?
What anguish did the Bible mean to her? When the minister
invited her to help him live into her no, she remembered that
when she was in fourth grade, the Sunday school made a big
ceremony of presenting her with a Bible of her very own.
They told her that she had earned this, and that this reward,
this Bible, was very special, because it could answer all her
questions, solve all her problems, make her feel right or
good when she felt wrong or bad. For her the Bible repre-
sented this great promise. But it also represented a promise
unkept—how ironic for the Bible to become the symbol of
broken covenant—because after the Sunday school gave her
this special gift and promise, in front of the church at the
altar (the place of holy ceremony and promise making), they
hardly ever mentioned the Bible again for years. The book
with all its promises stayed closed, and her questions and
fears, which were momentarily relieved by the promises of
the Bible, persisted, now covered by the scars of the broken
promises. That scar tissue and the wounds it covered were all
there in her no to Bible study at the age of thirty. So, too,
were other disappointments and broken promises for which
the Bible experience was a prototype: the promises she felt
when she entered into marriage, into motherhood, and into
adult roles in the church, as though these moments, too, promised, "Now all will be well." And, patently, all was not
made well by these moments. So these scars, too, these fears

of accepting any more promises, were in her no to Bible study.

And the minister could hear these groans; more important, he could let them speak for themselves, articulate themselves, pray for themselves, resolve themselves. No to Bible study meant recoil and protection from the false lure of promises nineteen years ago at the altar of one church, six years ago at the altar of another. It meant anger at the promise breakers and mistrust of all promise makers. It meant protective withdrawal from any lure of openness and investment of self—the more alluring, the more withdrawal—so if Bible study got a louder no than television commercials, that meant it was more tempting, more promising despite the disappointments. Her groaning no gave voice both to hope and to fear, in painful mix, to a longing to trust and to the felt risk of rage. The minister and the woman together entered into the no and let its groaning pour forth.

When the woman said, "You'd better skip me on this project," the minister did not reply with "You need it" or "I can always count on you" or "Are you upset about something these days?" or "Set a good example for others." Instead he said, "I can hear how unusually intense you are about this. The idea of Bible study must touch something sensitive."

The minister let the groaning quite literally speak for itself. He didn't try to articulate it or coach it by his own diagnosis or analysis. He didn't try to suppress it or heal it by offering remedies, such as "Fear not" or "Trust more." He didn't try to stand firmly on his own commitment to Bible study as the mode of ministry. He abandoned the posture of organizer and teacher of Bible study and accepted the emptied role of no posture, no ministry, only the forsaken role of fellow groaner. And as the groans spoke for themselves, they found their own focus, their own measure, their own limits, their own answer. The woman came to measure the past disappointments and to discover they *were* past. Her anger and fear had legitimate but limited targets: She could and should mistrust, but not everything; she could and should be leery of luring promises, but not absolutely. She felt the new surges of hope in discovering that her experience of mistrust and resistance, once focused and groaned through rather than scarred over and groaned about, was honest, was hers. It could be shared. Most remarkably, it did not separate her from God (or the Bible). For her groans, in their blend of yearning and forsakenness, hope and wrath, led both her and the minister to think of God's experience with his chosen, promised people; of Jesus' patient, painful experience with his earnest, floundering disciples. That made her groanings seem as meaningful, as grounded, as soaring as they were. Unthinking, but spontaneously responding, the minister turned to Hosea and to Romans 8. Astonishingly, the two of them were studying the Bible. But it didn't feel like "Bible study" for neither had come to this via their expectations of "Bible study" but rather had abandoned these expectations and had let the groanings lead them to the Bible. "Through our inarticulate groans the Spirit himself is pleading for us . . . in God's own way."

So the no *can* be heard as inarticulate groan and entered into and ministered through. But the groans of no, more than any other, tempt the minister to attribute articulateness, to hear the no literally and resoundingly, by hearing it only as though it were addressed to the minister and not issued out of the heart of the groaner, by hearing it as a sign of strength not of weakness, as an attack not a defense. For ministers have lodged self in ministry and have lodged ministry in particular projects and postures. But the lodging remains always precarious, for the ministry of the God discovered in the wilderness, in a stable, or on a cross can never be well lodged, much as ministers need it to be so. So no to a project provokes the minister's defense of self. Good defense requires precise targeting. So absence from church, from Bible study, or from the signatures on a petition—gestures that are likely to be meaningful but highly inarticulate groaning—become articulated by the minister into a precise, literal no so they can be contended with.

No to House Church

House churches, the gathering in a home for more intense exchange and more intimate worship than is possible in the church building, are increasingly important to ministers and people. They also raise significant ambivalences. To join a house church group, then to withdraw—that must be meaningful but inarticulate groaning. It must reflect the anguished mixture of a lifetime yearning for greater intimacy with others, with self, and with God, along with the fears that have previously precluded such intimacy. Everyone can articulate the desire to be closer to others, to one's own feelings and roots, or to God's love and direction; so minister and people can speak of wanting a house church and form one. But it is harder to speak of the nonwanting, though that is there, too. The misgivings of intimacy are less known, less articulate, so they get expressed more diffusely, less consciously, more behaviorally. One just leaves, walks away, avoids—it looks like no—to express the fears of letting down the usual roles and masks and of becoming more open and vulnerable; the apprehension of what new fullness and forthrightness will be expected if one opens up too much and too closely to other people or to God; the dread of the unwelcome scene in store if one looks too closely inward or lets others do so. Thus the ambivalence, which we sometimes rightly call awe, toward the promising and demanding heights, and depths, of awareness. Thus the built-in safeguards, such as anonymity or temporariness, that are provided for some occasions of sharing intense emotions

—the corner bar or the football stadium— or the safeguard of rows of seating that avoid face-to-face encounter that we build into bars and football stadiums and churches. When the structures have a no or an "out" built in, people can enter with less wariness, less need to fashion their own safeguarding no. What makes the house church attractive is its openness, its commitment to avoid protections against intimacy; and that is what makes it frightening.

To abandon a house church once joined, to "forget" its meetings, to sabotage its intimacy and openness with appeals for agenda and formality is a groaning, giving inarticulate sound or gesture to whatever fears this attractive yet disconcerting experience arouses. Personal and group censors seldom permit any more articulate expression. These groans, even though inarticulate, or perhaps especially because inarticulate, can be entered and shared and allowed to find their focus and resolution. Abandoned minister and abandoning member can together explore the "abandonment"—indeed, forget that they are "abandoned" and "abandoning"—and gradually discover the groaning that is in the abandonment and the distress that is in the groaning and the resolution that is in the distress.

"You were once so eager, and I guess still are, about the openness of our Friday night sessions," says the minister, inviting exploration, already trusted to mean just what is said and not to be suspected of a subtle, manipulative pep talk just to restore initial commitment and attendance. "So something about our group and the way we do things must be putting you off. Does it feel that way to you?"

"Yeah," the abandoner replies after a few more warm-up exchanges. "I know what it feels like to be open with you and I like that feeling in myself, and I felt that way at first on Friday nights. But now I just freeze when I get there. Even if I think about going, I feel my muscles tighten." (The body of a person, like the Body of Christ, is adept at inarticulate groans.)

"Like steeling yourself against a blow," the abandoned minister joins in, far past the separation of the abandonment.

Emboldened by the sharing and so less guarded, the minister's partner recalls: "Something about that one Friday when George talked so much, mostly about Ann, his wife, in fact, and I just didn't like what that was doing to her. I don't like to be part of something like that."

"You wouldn't want to do that." The minister keeps it close.

"Well, yes, I'm careful not to say things like that about Margie, especially in front of her."

"Careful?" The minister notes another form of a groaning no.

"Well, sure, of course, I sometimes feel like unloading stuff like that, but I just don't think that's right." So the distress in the groaning begins to show itself.

That's enough for one conversation; but after a few more conversations, the distress begins to find a resolution: "Well, probably some of those things I just do need to get off my chest. Maybe she can't hear them at first, and maybe I'm not always right about these things. But that's OK. It's a start."

So the abandonment of the house church leads to a fruit of the house church when that lead is followed. When the minister is able to be abandoned and to abandon her own posture as sponsor of the house church, then she can hear and follow the call to ministry that is in the abandonment. (Yes, in this case the minister was a woman. Were you startled? Was that surprise a groaning?)

But how much easier, how much more natural and understandable, to regard the abandonment as a resolute and articulate no and to attack and defend the no accordingly—to try to transform it back into yes—and to defend the self and the posture of ministry—to try to promote the house church because that's needed for the minister to feel "minister." "Think you can come back next week? You know we all promised to stick together on this." "Maybe we should serve refreshments, so people will feel more like coming." "I know you would like more structure to the evening, so it seems as if we get somewhere, but we all agreed we were going to try to stay open to the Spirit." The house church and its openness are good things, and why shouldn't good things be defended and promoted against resistance? Because that resistance is groaning, inarticulate groaning, and call to ministry is so often in groaning rather than in ongoing good things, in the inarticulate rather than the smoothly articulated, in surprise, even disruptive surprise, rather than the established. And because to attack the no is to strengthen it.

Nevertheless, this chapter needs to end by entering into the groaning of the minister not attacking it. The minister who has read this far wants to try to listen to and share people's groanings and can read through these examples with a nodding yes, or yes, I wish. Indeed, the minister undoubtedly wanted and knew how to listen and share long before reading these lines. But the no the reader adds to all of the above is the anguished recognition, which is mine fully as much as yours, that it doesn't easily work that way. "I can read or write these things and nod, but on the spot the stakes seem too high, the conditions are not right, I don't have time to think, or I feel off balance. So when someone crosses my path, resists and deflects what I'm about, I know later that was a signal I should have attended to and I feel guilty. But at the time I am angry and hurt and want to restore *my* balance, so I resent and rebuke or repress those groans and try to reshape the people to fit into their right places again in my programmed ministry. I know it's programmed, prefabricated, but that seems to be the way it is. When I read this stuff, I think I'd like to break out, should break out. But it doesn't happen. I can't." That indeed is also my own experience. If I could make it work as easily and automatically as I want, I wouldn't need to write all these pages to say how, and why. On the spot, I too frequently get lured into defensiveness or belligerence or stubborn professionalism and miss the message of what is being said to me. So all these pages are to help me be alert and trusting of the groaning, as groaning, as the place where God's Spirit acts.

3. Ministry in the Wilderness, Not Beyond It

Moses led Israel from the Red Sea out into the wilderness of Shur. For three days they travelled through the wilderness without finding water.

Exodus 15:22

Jesus was then led away by the Spirit into the wilderness, to be tempted by the Devil.

Matthew 4:1

The verses above are surely two of the most abrupt and realistic of the Bible, touching the heart of a minister's experience—the discovery that the minister is mostly in a wilderness, that ministry is in that wilderness.

In the first verse the Hebrew people have just made their decisive move, out of the captivity of Egypt and through the Red Sea, with all its strenuous terror. Now safely on the other side, they sing psalms of praise and thanksgiving, appropriate for having entered into the Promised Land, and they dance. For twenty-one verses of Chapter 15 of Exodus they celebrate. Then they turn and look around, and they are in a wilderness of untracked openness and debris of past forays, and they are thirsty and hungry and lost. They want to go back to Egypt. They spent forty years in that wilderness—as long as a minister's career.

In the second verse Jesus has just been baptized—surely the climax of a spiritual journey, a decisive step—and the heavens

37

have opened and pronounced him a most beloved son. The arduous and anguished journey to baptism is ended, and we are ready to see the path to ministry opened before him. Instead, the Spirit leads him into the wilderness, where he is hungry and lonely and sorely tempted to retreat back to the old ways, the display of spiritual power by the sure rules.

In their wilderness—and it seems it could only be so—the Hebrew people found their identity as a people, made contact with their God and found his support and direction for their lives. If the passage had been from captivity to the Promised Land, if the Red Sea had also been Jordan, as the people so fervently wished, they never would have discovered themselves to be the people of God. So also with Jesus: Could he have known himself, and be known, as Son of God had baptism catapulted easily into ministry?

In most of our spiritual and vocational pilgrimage, especially in professional ministry, we readily suppose that *a* decisive step is *the* decisive step, that liberation from obvious shackles that beset and besot us will launch us into that life and work of faith for which we so yearn while in captivity. While we are in Egypt, the only thing needful is to escape the Pharaoh and get across the formidable Red Sea. Then, over that hurdle, we relax, celebrate, ready to enjoy and till the promised land; and we are stunned to find ourselves stranded in a wilderness bleaker, less charted, and more littered with debris than the land of captivity we just escaped. So we make the breakthrough and answer the altar call or the call to ministry or the call to the first church or the call to the big church; and with all *that* painful uncertainty and searching anxiety and impatient waiting resolved, we look about and find ourselves in the midst of church or seminary or parish abounding in still more excruciating uncertainty and still more penetrating anxieties.

Even when we make the strenuous breakthrough and liberate ourselves from the constrictions of institution and narrow notions of "call" and ministry and parish, we discover ourselves in the midst of new constrictions and narrow notions, still finding a painful tracklessness and obstructing debris. The assistant who was going to free us from administrative hassles compounds them. The spontaneous prayer group that was freed, and freeing, of agendas and structures takes a lot of attention to keep it going. Our day off is unaccountably (or all too accountably) beset with urgent distractions. We may break out of the confines of the parish altogether. But if we go into experimental ministries, we find them all the more beset with trackless chaos demanding us to sponsor structure, or if we go into institutions like hospitals, we find them burdened with chaotic, ramshackle structure. Wilderness all. We want to go back to Egypt, sometimes back to the sure and simpler, though constricting, ways, sometimes at least back to the sure and simpler vision we had in Egypt of how it was going to be. We try hard sometimes to impose on the wilderness our Egyptian vision of the Promised Land, but it proves no map for the wilderness, only more constriction and obstacle. There is no way back to Egypt and no way forward to the Promised Land, except by allowing the wilderness to yield up its own tracks and treasures.

Perhaps the rhythms are seen more easily in smaller moments of ministry. Crossing the Red Sea—what seems, until afterward, *the* decisive step—may be the fashioning of a sermon, the organizing of a committee, the making of an appointment for counseling. The recalcitrance of text and ideas finally yields to a coherent sermon. The lethargy of members and minister yields to a meeting in which all are agreed to plan Project X. The awkwardness of minister and the resistance of counselee are finally overcome by what seems to the minister a clear mutual commitment to "sit down together and face these things." The Red Sea has been crossed and ministry has been launched! Then the minister looks around and finds that they are in the wilderness: The sermon is misheard and attracts only superficial reaction, and that walk down the aisle afterward seems a longer and narrower passage than through the Red Sea. The committee meeting gets bogged down in delaying wrangling. The counselee comes and shows intense and ingenious resistance to facing serious issues: "I don't quite remember what bothered me so much when we made this appointment."

To me it is as clear as the discoveries in the Biblical wildernesses that ministry truly begins when the wilderness is fully entered, even, especially, when the wilderness is a disruption of the expected ministry. The rebuff to sermon, to committee project, or to counseling commitment *is* a rebuff, and is painful and frustrating to the minister—so long as the minister's head is back in Egypt with the memory of the expectations acquired there. The minister may well be tempted—it is the most standard response—to recall people to the Egypt of the earlier contract and expectations: "But you *said* you wanted me to preach and implied you would take me seriously. But you *said* you were committed to this committee project, or this counseling process! Now make good on your contract and stop leaving me stranded!" "Recall and live up to your initial visions and commitments, the plans made back in Egypt."

But the rebuff is also a genuine response, and it calls to be taken seriously and responded to, not denied and ploughed over. The rebuff is a step forward, even if into the wilderness. There is nurture and direction to be found in the wilderness, a message in the mess, manna in the mania. If seminaries are arenas of doubt and struggle not oases of quiet faith, what lessons are to be learned in that struggle that take one beyond the expectations of faithful serenity and settlement? What does the wilderness have to teach that would never be found in the Promised Land envisioned in Egypt? If the parish, too, is the arena of unwelcome, unexpected, even petty, struggle and contention quite unlike the established people of God one may have thought promised, what lesson, what summons, is to be heard in *that* wilderness? If experimental nonparish ministry, or administrative assistant, or prayer group, or day off flounder on unexpected administrative scurrying, what is the lesson therein? *Why* do minister and people seem to attract or need or tolerate such intrusive busyness? What need for cover or crutch may be signaled by this busyness and may therefore be calling new ministry either to self or to others? A casual response to a sermon may well reflect ambivalence toward the message, and ambivalence signals an emotionally important reaction. So also with the committee wrangling and the counseling resistance. If a topic seems so hard to remember or to talk about, it must touch something deep. The very struggle to speak and keep in focus rather than suppress and blur is an important one, to be heard and joined by the minister. When that is done, then the journey is begun.

No one knows where it will lead. Frequently the old ways and old visions of Egypt will seem more than attractive, for the present wilderness is real. The possibility of discovery does not make the wilderness attractive or easy. It *is* uncharted and full of debris, stumbling, and hunger. The suffering is real. The minister *does* feel stranded and emptied and alone and lost. That's the way it is!

Lured into the Wilderness

Joseph Fischer had a special reason to feel annoyed and devastated—"wildernessed"—by Janet Snyder's no. Only the day before she had not only said yes to his ministry, she had said please. Janet had said that she had urgent problems to discuss about her marriage and needed to see Joe immediately. It was an important breakthrough, or break-out—out of

Egypt and through the Red Sea—for her to open herself this much to reflection and counseling, for Joe to feel he had elicited this much trust and rapport. He didn't hesitate to take the trip through the Red Sea to the Promised Land. He arranged a time inconvenient to him in order to accommodate her. Then they both discovered that she had little or nothing to say.

To be lured by promises of being needed and then to be stranded is the most devastating of experiences for a minister. And when done at the hands of a woman, it is the most devastating of experiences for a man. More stark Biblical images than the wilderness may suggest themselves: Samson at the mercy of the seductive then disempowering Delilah. When men ministers speak of the church as "she," they may be recognizing or setting the stage for their feelings that the church is seducer and castrater. "Give me your best, I need it and want it," she first seems to say. But that soon becomes, "Give me your best, I only want to take it away from you." Yet I still dare to ask ministers to pick themselves up off the floor after such a wipe-out and to attend to the needs of the one who is wreaking such devastation; not just to *over*look the attack but to *in*-look it, to look into the wilderness for its own tracks, even when the wilderness feels more like engulfing jungle than bleak desert.

Janet Snyder was middle-aged. Her last children had left home, and she was vigorously experimenting with ways to invest her obvious energies and talents. She was increasingly active in the church and was sampling a new career with a part-time job and talked of returning to school. Two or three times at coffee hours and before and after committee meetings she had made remarks to Joe about strain between her and her husband. She talked of disagreements, of feeling constricted by some of his expectations that she stay home. "I do have to live my own life, and he is not the center of it, even if he thinks he is." Joe listened well. One day she called Joe and said she must see him as soon as possible. Her tone was annoyed and strong, and she said "I must be making some decisions soon." Joe felt her grievances against her husband were coming to a head. She seemed urgently to need to unburden herself. He agreed to cut short his supper the next night and to see her before a committee meeting at the church.

Janet started out a bit awkwardly. "I have been wondering all day just what I would say to you; I wonder really why I want to see you." Such a slow windup was appropriate and standard for any difficult conversation, and Joe waited. But the windup persisted, and the pitch never came. Janet did talk about her marriage: She made an inventory of her husband's fine qualities and did not happen to include any other qualities. She described with unalloyed appreciation his support for her new career, how he had helped her to find a job, and how he was offering her a new car if she needed it. "He is so sweet and so supportive." She reaffirmed her commitment to the marriage and her intention that any new career not interfere with it. Joe recognized this dilemma of balancing marriage and a career— of being fair to husband and to self—as a real problem, and he tried to help Janet think through these questions, to clarify her priorities, and to be aware of risks and options. But he also recognized that this was not an urgent problem; the feelings she had expressed the day before, of being aggrieved and on the brink, were not present in this conversation. She had called him to help her deal with a crisis that she was not now experiencing, or at least not talking about.

Joe could have focused on the no. He could have called Janet's attention to his own setup and letdown and her role in producing it. "Do you often lead on men in this way, then let them down? Does this illustrate something that is a difficulty in your marriage?" This is one way for a minister to make some use of his hurt, his personal wilderness. It is a kind of psychological inquiry, a common one, but certainly not the way recommended in this book. It turns the attack back on Janet. It makes her feel wrong or sick for saying no. It does not invite her to explore her no, only to explore his hurt and to feel guilty for it. It is, in the common way of men relating to women, defining the episode in terms of *his* experience, assuming that disruptions in the situation are due to the woman's defects or disease. It's not much different from the complainings of the Hebrew people to Moses: Now see what you have done to us. Psychological sophistication encourages this kind of defense by diagnosis; this book does not. The no is a signal of distress, a clue to be explored; it is not itself the distress, except perhaps for the minister. For the minister to focus literally on the no and take it at face value is to understand it only for what it means to the minister. In this case Janet is not saying no; Joe hears no. The no is the clue to ask what she *is* saying.

Joe could have tried to recall Janet to her yes. He could have reminded her of the agenda she once had for this meeting and asked her to stick to it. He had kept to his contract by arranging the time; she should keep hers. He could have coached and prompted her: "You said you wanted to get together and talk about grievances and about decisions. Let's do it."

Instead, he called attention to the discrepancy as such and made it clear that it was a discrepancy they shared. The yes and the no were both valid and important, and so was the discrepancy between them. This discrepancy must have a meaning that was important to both of them. In any case, it was a discrepancy they now shared. He was curious about it and respectful of it, and of Janet.

"You seem to be in a different mood today from yesterday," Joe said to Janet. "Yesterday you were agitated and had some intense things pressing on you. Tonight you seem calmer and seem to be searching for something to focus on." Can such a remark be uttered and be heard as descriptive and not as judgmental, as an expression of curiosity not of scolding, as an expression of something they now share rather than as something that makes them adversaries? Can Janet feel that Joe is scratching his head not pointing his finger? Most important, can Joe successfully invite them to be open to what is new rather than governed by what is old, to be hearing the call to ministry that is in the very disruption of the old contract of ministry? No less than the Hebrew people with Moses and no less than Jesus, Janet and Joe are in a new wilderness together. It is a wilderness promising new affirmations. Somewhere in the very fact that Janet and Joe's conversation is different today from what they expected, and more wandering, there are clues to insight and to healing; but the affirmations are not yet visible and cannot become so until the expectations of the past, even of yesterday, are severed, their sovereignty overthrown. They really are in a wilderness, and only by facing that fully can they discover the life and call and ministry that awaits them in it.

Joe wants to face starkly that they are in a new wilderness, that they have left behind the expectations and covenants of yesterday. "It hardly seems now worth rushing our suppers for." The real risk is that he will sound judgmental not descriptive, that he will seem to be complaining (emphasizing the no) or coaching (trying to return to the yes) not really accepting where they *are*—in the wilderness. What he wants is to invite them both to leave that old contract and its debris well behind and to explore, together and in trust, the new dilemma in which they find themselves. The peril of communication lies in the fact that the dilemma is defined partly by the disparity from the previous expectation and contract; calling attention to such disparity ordinarily implies rebuke and recall to contract. "This conversation doesn't have the urgency and focus we both expected when we made the special appointment." Such a remark ordinarily signals rebuke. Can he really mean it, and can she really hear it as a call to explore this new wilderness for its new but as yet undisclosed signs of hope and of direction?

In a sudden moment of unexpected abandonment, unforeseen wilderness, can Joe really mean what he firmly believes as a more general principle? Can he make convincing in this incident what may seem quite plausible only in more sweeping rhetoric? If Joe Fischer really believes it, can he say it in a way that Janet Snyder can hear? If at first he feels her, though unconsciously, as a Delilah luring and then emasculating him, can he regard her and make her feel regarded, as a fellow pilgrim? From the pulpit—above it all—Joe can believe and preach that God reveals himself and calls and guides and supports in the wilderness and the brokenness of life, in the debris of old covenants, in the wandering of wilderness. He can warn how tempting and also how ultimately frustrating it is to want to return from the wilderness back to Egypt, to the safety of former guidelines and habits and covenants. But what if one finds a real wilderness in one's own life? What if one has hurried supper to meet a crisis and finds no crisis, only a woman who says, "I wonder why it was I needed to see you?" Then Joe really knows what it is like to want to revert to the old covenant and to make it govern and redeem the occasion: out of the wilderness and back into Egypt. Turn these stones back into bread. "Let's get back to business, Janet."

When we take any decisive step in ministry and in faith, we often expect it to be *the* decisive step, or perhaps we would never take it. Accepting God's call and entering seminary; accepting the church's call and entering its ministry; making the pastoral call that enters intimately into a family's life; making the telephone call that gets a project organized and launched; answering the altar call that offers one new life—all of these decisive steps seem to be *the* decisive steps, themselves risky and difficult. Once they are accomplished, one may well join the Hebrew people in their psalms after crossing the Red Sea. "The Lord is my refuge and my defense, he has shown himself my deliverer" (Exod. 15:2). And one can even read, with some understanding and identification, the climactic verse of the baptism: "And a voice from heaven was heard saying, 'This is my Son, my Beloved . . .' " (Matt. 3:17). Those calls are so strenuous that once the connection is made, the yes said on both sides, then the path of ministry and faith seems to lie smoothly ahead.

We enter into the disrupted home on our pastoral calls, with visions of bringing clarity and reconciliation to that disrupted family, and having been invited and welcomed to do just that. But instead we are met with a trackless suspicion (anything new may disrupt the precarious equilibrium) and so much debris of past battles and failures at reconciliation that all paths seem obstructed. Yet ministry, in the form of insight and reconciliation, is to be found only by exploring deeply within these suspicions and obstacles not by trying to get past them.

The Janet who says no to the previous contract is not less than the Janet who said yes to it, though that is how it feels to Joe, who wants to bring her back "up" to the contract. The Janet who says no is *more* than the Janet who said yes. She is a new Janet, someone to get newly acquainted with. For there is substance, texture, richness, and much meaning and guidance in the no. In the no is where Janet is most presently and immediately living, in the no is where she is most emphatically and energetically addressing the important matters of her life. One need hardly be surprised that the address is resistant and ambivalent and disruptive; most serious attention to serious matters is.

So Joe did not need to stop and mock at the apparent no to

something old. He wanted to get acquainted with the meaning of this new response, and he supposed Janet did too. In the no is where she was most emphatically and energetically addressing the important matters of her life. Joe did not know what these were. They were in the no, obscured by it. But they *were* in the no—in the know?—their presence signaled by the no. So he called their attention to the no, looking squarely at it as the no it was, so as to identify it and to accept it as a signal.

"You seem to be in a different mood today from yesterday. Yesterday you were agitated and had some intense things pressing on you. Tonight you seem calmer and seem to be searching for something to focus on. It hardly seems now worth rushing our suppers for." He meant to accept the no as a signal of something important in her and not as a rebuke that she had said no. He really wanted to focus on the no, on today's calmness and rambling after yesterday's urgency, as what was real and important and meaningful. That is what they were sharing and what they could talk about as important clue and path. He did not want to focus on yesterday's yes, on the agitation and the "intense things," as though they were what was important, and as though they were not having meaningful conversation until they could return to yesterday's conversation, yesterday's contract.

If Janet had been made to feel defensive, rebuked for the no or recalled to the contract, then she might have responded by denying the no ("I *am* talking about important problems in my marriage") or explaining the no in trivial ways ("I guess I'm tired at the end of a long day") or denying the contract ("I wasn't so sure what was bothering me yesterday either") or explaining away the contract in trivial terms ("I guess my busy schedule just made me tense yesterday. I should have had a good drink and not bothered you").

But instead of feeling rebuked or recalled, she felt invited to explore this discrepancy as of interest and of import. "Yes,

I do feel more subdued tonight, less adventurous, less like exploring new things, and more like settling down in a nest and being comfortable." She accepted Joe's reflection of her changed mood and sharpened it with her own words. These sharper words represented a new step inward, toward meaning, from the superficial calmness where they started.

Ready to take still another step, Joe picked up some of these sharper words and kept them focused on their immediate situation, still on the no she had said to their original contract. "Yesterday it seemed you wanted to spend time with me to strategize, explore, maybe even hold a war council, but tonight it feels more like you want me to help you build a nest and huddle in it and count your blessings."

"I do have so many blessings, don't I," Janet conceded, acknowledging that he touched her mood correctly. "A good marriage, a husband who cares about what I'm doing and supplies the money to do it. Just this morning he was asking me closely about how I was going to spend the day."

And then, while Joe was silent, Janet reflected on the discrepancy that he had pointed to and that she had begun to hear in her own remarks. "But you are right; yesterday I was feeling myself more of an independent person, not so much just his wife, and I was feeling some restrictions and some anger in the marriage, not just comfort. Yesterday it felt a little more like a prison and not just a nest."

"And yesterday you would have been annoyed not reassured by his close scrutiny of your day's schedule." Joe tried to show that he was thinking her thoughts with her.

"Yes, yesterday I was wanting to be more of an independent woman and even be willing to face some of the things in my marriage that were perhaps holding me back." And then Janet added with a sigh, "But all that seems lost today."

"No I don't think it's lost. I think it's covered up." Joe shared with Janet explicitly his conviction that the no was more not less than the yes, that the seeming "loss" of the spirit of yesterday was itself a meaningful event. "I think you still just as much want to be the independent woman and to face difficult issues in your marriage. For some reason, today you *also* seem to want to play the role of the comfortably married woman." The particular contours of the no were becoming clearer to both of them.

"Why would I feel that way especially today?" She accepted the well-focused invitation to look for meaning in the change.

"I don't know." Joe really *didn't* know. He only had the conviction that her change, her no, was a signal to something meaningful in her life. And he had tried to say so clearly and acceptingly.

"Well, there was an awkward thing that happened this morning." Janet let her mind go into her marriage and look for clues. "I was up late last night writing some letters. I have some friends who are very important to me to keep in touch with. And when he got up this morning he noticed that I had left the desk light on. And he was furious. I know how important it is to him to keep lights turned off, and I should have been more careful."

"You sound like a bad girl," Joe said, keeping the focus on her subdued, self-effacing posture of the day, which apparently began with this morning episode.

"Well, he was very angry."

"And that really got to you this time. Sometimes I have heard you talk about his fussing in a different perspective, as a restriction you resented. But this time you have it that he is right and you are wrong." Again, Joe's strategy was to focus on the discrepancy, on what was new and, although disrupting and unwelcome, probably very meaningful.

"He was shouting in a way that I don't think I have heard before." His anger had really frightened her. "I didn't know what he might do."

"You were afraid he might hit you?" Joe probed.

"No, no . . . but he might leave me." Janet suddenly realized this as she blurted it out. And she was suddenly sobbing with the realization. "That's it, he has seemed so patient and accepting, but if all that anger is there, perhaps it's been building, and he just may do something about it."

"And that would leave you abandoned." Joe could understand such anguish especially keenly.

Then the conversation went on, usefully and intensely and intimately about Janet's fears of being left alone, both by her husband and by others earlier in her life, and of the desperate anxiety such rejection and such loneliness raised for her. It became a crucial and valuable counseling session about fears that frequently afflicted and immobilized her. These fears and the possibility of dealing with them in counseling were discovered precisely by attention to the effects of these fears as they showed up in her no to Joe, her repudiation of the earlier contract. Janet was immobilized from meeting her own and Joe's expectations of what their after-supper session would be, just as she was frequently immobilized from doing other things she wanted to do and for precisely the same reasons. In her "nesting" posture with Joe there was a small sample of an important reaction that was frequent in her life. By paying attention to the fact that it was meaningful to her, even without knowing that meaning and by ignoring the disruptive meaning it had for him, Joe was able to help her see and deal with something important in herself.

Janet *was* bringing her full self to Joe for counseling. The full self happened to be even fuller than their first contract had anticipated. By paying attention to that new fullness, as disruptive and disconcerting as it was, Joe was able to be a counselor to Janet as she was. They both had had expectations when they made their appointment—expectations formed in Egypt—of how they could be counselor and counselee for each other. If they had stuck with those expectations and tried to fulfill them, they would have become battlers, a scolder and a defender. By giving up their expectations of how they would be counselor and counselee and by dealing directly with the new wilderness in which they found themselves, they were able to be counselee and counselor in more profound and meaningful ways.

4. Turning the Other Cheek to Take a Good First Look

You have learned that they were told, "Eye for eye, tooth for tooth." But what I tell you is this: Do not set yourself against the man who wrongs you. If someone slaps you on the right cheek, turn and offer him your left. If a man wants to sue you for your shirt, let him have your coat as well. If a man in authority makes you go one mile, go with him two. Give when you are asked to give; and do not turn your back on a man who wants to borrow.

Matthew 5:38–42

Come downstairs for a while, to the junior high Sunday school class, for a fresh interpretation of the teaching from Matthew, and discover still another restatement of the perspective of this book.

I ask a girl to start walking across the room with her eyes shut, as though she were blind. "First we will do it the old way," I say, starting to walk across her path and timing myself so that she jostles me. Looking straight ahead and never at her, I shout, "Watch where you're going," and I push her away with my elbow. A push for a push. My stride, momentarily interrupted, goes on. She stumbles about, chagrined.

"That is what Jesus called the old way; now let us see the new way." I have the "blind" girl start out again. I time it so that I am again jostled. But this time I turn my cheek, my whole head in fact, so as to look at her. I have been pushed as before, interrupted, and thrown off stride. But this time I turn and see *why* I have been pushed. "Oh you are blind," I say. "May I help you?" I take her hand and move alongside her.

"Now, you do it," I say. "I'll be the Sunday paperboy, and I haven't delivered your paper by 9:30 this morning. You call me up. First the old way." I sit in the corner and make my hands into a telephone.

"Where is my paper!?" "Why are you so lazy!?" The class enjoys getting angry at me, and they catch on to the eye-for-an-eye. If I let them down, they will try to respond in kind. "Don't expect to get paid for the paper if you can't get it here on time." "I'm going to stop having you deliver the paper, and I'll go out and get it myself."

"Now try it by turning the other cheek and looking more closely at me," I say. They know how to do this, too, though perhaps with an exaggeration that may come from little practice and few models. "Are you sick today? Is there anything we can do?" "Maybe the papers didn't get delivered to you. You must have a lot of people getting mad at you. And it's not even your fault." The class is already hearing the call to action that is in the disruption. Not the eye-for-an-eye retaliatory response; that is easy, automatic, and not very interesting or demanding. Rather, they respond to the call to be vigorous, imaginative, forthcoming, effective—the call that arises in looking more closely at the disruption. To turn the other cheek and take a good first look, and then to deal with what you see, is a posture not of weakness but of strength. It is not abjectly submitting to a situation but vigorously moving into it. These junior high students delight in that call to action.

"Now let's all do it," I say, and I ask David to be a substitute teacher in his school the next day. "And I'll be a kid who tries to take advantage of you." I start tapping my pencil under the table and shuffling my feet; he rises to the bait, shrilly: "Who's doing that? Stop it this minute, or you'll have to go to the principal." He overreacts, and to his overreaction the whole class now responds predictably. There is furtive pencil tapping and foot shuffling and an occasional low whistle from every corner of the room where David is not looking. David continues to overreact, the substitute teacher losing control and desperate, "Who did that? Stop that! Hands out on the table! Go stand in the corner!" The situation deteriorates into a confrontational brawl, which I have to end prematurely and rapidly, for the adults upstairs in the worship service would never understand that *this* disruptive noise was meaningful, that we had just acted out a confrontational episode not different, except in explicitness, from many they engage in in the life of the church.

"But now let's do it the other way." I tap my pencil and shuffle my feet. After David overreacts shrilly, I interrupt: *"Why* is he getting so uptight over a little pencil tapping. Most teachers wouldn't let me bait them that much." Turn the other cheek and take a good first look. The class delights in this call to action more than they did in the mindless automatic pencil tapping, for now they are challenged to be resourceful and forthcoming, to take David the teacher, and hence themselves, more seriously. If they were ministers, we could even say that they were being recalled to the center of their ministry. "It's hard to be a substitute." "It's hard to be a teacher." (Why?) "It's not really your class. . . . You're afraid the kids won't like you . . . no, you're afraid the principal won't like you. Yeah, the principal had to come in the other day and take over our music class from the substitute teacher. Some of the kids felt good, but I felt sorry for the teacher. . . . If you're a substitute, you don't even know if you're going to have a class till they call you at breakfast. . . . Yeah, then you hope you get a better class the next day. . . ." People, junior high students or ministers or anyone else, don't need a lot of coaching to see how it is with others. They simply need the invitation to turn the other cheek and take a good look.

"My name is Jim," I tell David the teacher, wondering whether the others want to join me in making a more personal address to the plight of the substitute they have just identified. Some do: "And I'm Dora, and we're glad you are our teacher today. . . . The principal doesn't usually come around until after lunch. . . . We're supposed to be on page thirty-six, and it's Billy's turn to recite. . . . Don't tell the teacher what to do, maybe he has a different plan. . . ." These students might never bring this off under the restraints of a real classroom with a real substitute, but they clearly have it within them, and it comes out easily in the freedom of the role playing here. They do know how to respond to the call to action, the call to ministry.

One more instance, the most touching of all to me: "I am a father," I say. "You be my children. This is Sunday, and I am very busy today. But let's do something together next week. What do you want to do?" "Go with us to a baseball game," one blurts out, and I readily agree. "That's a promise."

"Now it's next Sunday." I set the stage as I then busy myself, head in hands, with a lot of papers on the table in front of me. Patient silence, and then, "Aren't you going to take us to the ball game?" I stay busy with my papers. "Aren't you going to keep your promise?" Finally, I speak without looking up, "I have an awful lot of work I have to do today. Can we get together and do something next Sunday?" "But you promised for today!" The expressions of grief and disappointment are intense. But there is no belligerent eye-for-an-eye reaction.

Then in a lull, Arthur quietly speaks up from across the room, "Why is your work so important to you, Daddy?"

The moisture in my eyes is real as I carry on the role for a bit. "My boss may get mad at me if I don't get these things ready by tomorrow morning." And so on.

Arthur did turn the other cheek and look squarely into his disappointment to find a meaning, a point of contact, a call to action. This is a true story; it did happen in a junior high Sunday school class.

But let the students move out and let some ministers come in for a seminar on ministry.

Let us reenact the first scene, a blind person bumping a striding person. Ministry is like that: deflected striding. One is purposefully and steadfastly striding on course—the stride is proper, for the set course is a dedicated response to a real call —then there is disruption. One can respond eye-for-an-eye: With eye and stride fixed firmly on the original call, the disruption is only deflection and itself must be disrupted—push back and keep going on course. Who can fault such steadfastness and discipline? Jesus is not fixing fault when he says, "But what I tell you is. . . ." But one can look into the disruption for the new call within it, "Oh, you are blind, can I help you?"

To be a minister is to receive blows knocking one off course and into ministry. But Jesus tells not just about blows but about having garments stripped off and about forced marches. And ministry is like that, too. Still more painful than blows and deflections, and containing still more urgent calls, may be the disruptions that are abandonments, when someone or something moves away not against. For this, let us stage the role playing a bit differently. A string of stepping stones is laid down across the room, cardboards, since this is still a Sunday school classroom. I will play the role of minister and start striding along the path. Just ahead of me you, playing the role of lay people, pull away one or two of the stones. If your timing is right, as it usually is with most ministers, you will pull away the stepping stones just when my foot is poised in mid-air, with my weight already committed to it, and suddenly there is no place to receive my step and my weight. "Stop, thief!" I cry, jarred and off balance and frightened and angry. I may be especially frustrated because your thievery is legalized and proper—Jesus has the coat removed by legal suit—unassailable by ordinary redress. Eye-for-an-eye, I grab for the stones and anything else you may be carrying: Undo the disruption, pay for your crime, and let me continue on course. This is what the episode means to me, if I construe my call rigidly and inflexibly.

Or I can turn the other cheek and take a good look at what the episode means to you: Do you need the stones for building a shelter? Perhaps I should help you carry some more from my path. If you take my coat because you *need* it, perhaps you need my cloak as well. Do you take the stones because you are angry at me or at what I represent? Perhaps I am called to stand by and to explore that anger with you, its roots and its targets, and to share it. Do you take the stones because you feel helpless and alone and are claiming attention? Perhaps I should not only run after you the one mile it takes to catch you and the stones but also go with you the second mile to your home while I catch the meaning of your action and give you the attention you need and deserve.

To touch still another experience of disruption becoming ministry things must be staged still differently in the classroom. Along with blows and abandonments there are forced marches. Again, I stride purposefully and steadfastly toward my goal across the room, when two of you close in and shoulder me off course and along a course of your choosing. You can call yourselves bishops or office secretaries or parents of high schoolers or pulpit committee members or altar guild members or panhandlers from the street or alcoholics from the board of deacons or wealthy contributers with pet peeves or anyone else who has ideas about how I should conduct my ministry and the power to impose them.

Eye-for-an-eye, I will resist your shouldering as best I can, push against your pushing, though perhaps furtively; when you tire or lapse, I will dart back to my original course until you come and shoulder me away again. That is the usual pattern of ministers, resisting the resistance and sticking to their agenda as best they can.

"But what I tell you is this. . . ." If your path deflects from mine, then not only does it deflect from mine; it is also a path of your choosing and must have some meaning for you (other than contradicting mine). I will never know that meaning by fighting for my path against yours. Nor will I ever know that meaning if I let myself just passively be carried along by you. (Going the second mile, like turning the other cheek and giving away the cloak, can be submissive and passive and compliant, can be a yielding up of self and an end of initiative and of ministry. Or it can be, as the junior high students quickly learned with delight, a mode of active investment of self, searching and challenging.) I can learn the meaning if I make the effort—and it is an effort, a call, a challenge—to go *with* you, to pace my stride to yours, to see the goals for which you are heading, to hear what you say about the path you have chosen rather than just muttering to myself that it is a detour from mine. I can *choose* to follow the call in the disruption, even in the shouldering and in the forced march. And with that choice, that response to the call, goes investment.

Pain is not the mark of ministry. One is not a minister *because* one receives a blow, has a coat stolen or a firm stepping stone dislodged, or is forced to go on a detour. One does not court these disruptions nor count them as certifying ministry. The minister is not called to suffer, or at least that is not the call pointed to in this book. The call is *in* the suffering, when it happens, especially when the suffering is the disruption of ministry. To be sure, the Christian believes that God's suffering, in Christ, is redemptive, and perhaps that redemptive act gives charter to ministry. But the theological charter for ministry relied on here has more to do with God's creativity and his commitment to history, especially its surprises. The God who called out of the burning bush and was found in a mean manger and in all the other nooks and crannies of history, in the byways passed over by human structures and preferences— that is the God who still calls men and women by his surprising creativity, opening up wonders and mission where people least expect it. The theological charter relied on here has more to do with God's transcendence of human structures and agendas and designs. The God who refused to be confined to a temple or to a set of laws, to the expectations of disciples or Palm Sunday crowds or crucifying enemies, to the structures of thought or of organization throughout the church's history —that is the God who refuses to be confined to any definition of ministry or agenda for the day, however valid and right that definition or agenda may be.

There is, indeed, an eerie link between agendas and suffering. The tighter the agenda, the more painful is any disruption of it. Disruption does not produce the suffering. Disruption is only disruption; it inflicts pain only if there is a tautness unready for the blow. The tense body is damaged by the blow that the relaxed body rebounds from. It is undue reliance on the law that makes the law, or its breaking, damaging.

Calling may be suffered for; suffering is not called for. The easy misunderstanding that suffering is *called* for, that it is certification of ministry, leads people to seek the suffering and to suppose that simple submission, meek compliance, passive acceptance of blows or of abandonment or of forced marches is sufficient as ministry. Those who seek and welcome the suffering miss the meaning *in* the disruption fully as much as those who resist the disruption. One can meekly comply with the forced march or one can stubbornly resist it and in either case miss ministry. Or one can choose to join it and find ministry.

Resistance to the Bible

"If someone slaps you on the right cheek. . . ." Let us return to role playing. I will be a minister wanting to lead Bible study on the verses that head this chapter. And you be a person who interrupts with the tired joke Samuel Clemens told. He found only one verse in the Bible that spoke to him, Matthew 5:41: "And whosoever shall compel thee to go a mile, go with him twain." Eye-for-an-eye, I can counter your irreverence and your irrelevance with my own. I can push against your pushing, "Well, he can make that joke work only by using the Elizabethan English of the King James Bible, and we are not using that." Or I could meekly submit to your blow, your forced march: "That's a good story, does anybody have any others?" Or "Mark Twain was an interesting person; that reminds me of. . . ."

"But what I tell you is. . . ." To find whatever call there is in your disruption, I must neither resist your push nor yield to it. Instead, I want to turn the other cheek and look more closely at you and what you have said. "What makes you think of that right now?" I ask rather directly. And if you are used to my style and trust me, as perhaps can be the case in this role playing, you may come back with something like, "That always struck me as pretty irreverent." And, after a couple more exchanges: "I always wondered how a great man like that could get away with being so irreverent about the Bible." Perhaps I capture your mood if I reply, "And maybe *you* are tempted sometimes to feel the same way about the Bible." If this really is an issue of concern to you, and if you are willing to pursue it, and if I am willing to leave my original agenda behind, then we have together discovered a way to spend our time in profitable and energetic search for the meaning of the Bible in our lives. We have, together, found a call to ministry in the midst of your disruption of the agenda to which I had once felt so firmly called.

Defrocking in the Narthex

"If a man wants to sue you for your shirt. . . ." So much for one kind of blow a minister receives. Now let's see, in another role play, how it feels to be stripped or to have the rug pulled out from under. Suppose you, a woman, are a minister who has just finished a sermon and is greeting people at the door, and I am a person who is not used to hearing you—or any woman —preach. "I enjoyed your sermon today. . . . (pause) . . . Your voice really carried well, so we could hear you quite easily. . . . (turning to the person next in line) . . . Doesn't she look attractive in that robe?" How gently I strip off your coat, peel your ministry from you: first by ignoring what you said, second by treating you like a child from whom I expect little compe- tence, and third—most literally, stealing your garment—by treating a symbol of your office, your robe, as anything but a symbol of your office. It is a devastating putdown, delivered regularly and benevolently to women clergy by those who have trouble seeing women as clergy.

You have every reason and every motive to defend yourself and to respond vigorously and in kind, eye-for-an-eye. You can treat me, icily or gently, as the bigot that I am: "Do you make comments to men ministers like that, or only women? Maybe if I were a man you could have heard what I was saying in my sermon." You have been jolted, and you jolt back; aff- ronted and confronted, and you confront back. It is an appro- priate, and perhaps a necessary, response. But it is eye-for-an- eye. It is also I-for-an-I, responding to my self-protective, mildly emotional outburst with one of your own, dealing with my remark in terms of what it means to you personally. You have heard it said, many times if you have been in women's groups discussing these matters, that you should respond eye-for-an-eye, and perhaps you should. But Jesus says there is another way.

Some may misunderstand this other way to be one of docile submission, playing the servant and suffering in silence. You could simply swallow the affront, absorb the jolt: "I am glad you enjoyed the sermon." Or you could, even more compliantly, play along in the role to which my bigotry has assigned you: "I am so glad that you could hear me. I was afraid my voice might not be big enough for this large church." Or, even more compliantly to the point of caricature and mocking—whether of yourself or of me—"Yes, I do like to look nice in the pulpit. Maybe that's one reason I became a minister."

Whether you ignore my affront or collude in it, you are abandoning ministry even as you abandon self and, in a very important sense, abandon me. You leave the initiative up to me and roll with it, either passively or more actively, but without ever looking at the me that is taking this initiative. Such submissiveness, no less than an eye-for-an-eye retort, takes my remarks for what they mean to you not for what they mean to me, not as an avenue by which you might reach back toward me and minister. Ministry does not come by docility alone or by suffering alone, and it seems incomplete to think that this is what Jesus was recommending. Certainly it is not what I am recommending. Withholding the self-protective retort may be a sacrifice that is a necessary condition of ministry, but it does not constitute ministry. Withholding the retort saves room for ministry, but it does not save people. Ministry comes, or doesn't, in the room thus made.

If both retort and retreat are different versions of the I-for-an-I that somehow denies the I in each of us by covering up, then perhaps the alternative can be called I-for-you, in which you open yourself as you want to open me. You may turn the other cheek and take a good look—or in this case a good listen

—at me and at what you have heard, and you may speak about what you see and hear. Perhaps you say, "You seem surprised that you could hear me so well." Or "You must not be used to having a woman preacher." "Not used to" is a gentle recognition of feelings that might more accurately, but not more usefully, be labeled as ambivalent, bewildered, confused, distressed, even fearful.

I can feel some of this recognition and concern and respond accordingly, at least with some willingness to concede that I do have some feelings about the matter. "Well, it does seem a little different." Then suddenly realizing that you might suppose—accurately—that some of the feelings were not all positive, I quickly add, "But I like it."

Ignoring the cover, and responding to the opening, you might simply inquire, "Different in what ways?" (You might go on to speculate for me about the differences I find, but I feel more comfortable that you don't. I feel more like expressing myself if you stand back and leave room for me.)

Even so, I still come at it gradually. "I guess I'm just more used to hearing a man's voice doing the preaching."

"You are sure that a man's voice is strong enough and that it will get through." You remind me of the way I first put it but choose words and tones that leave room for more meaning than simple acoustics.

I accept the invitation, but indirectly. "I guess you *have* had all the training, haven't you? And you certainly seem like you know what you're talking about."

"But it is harder, somehow, to be sure that a woman has the word of God to say." You echo the implied misgivings and then go on to help me identify, and to share, the yearning that the misgivings reflect. "And it is pretty important to try to get the word straight."

"You never quite know what to believe these days, and it is so easy to make mistakes." And I am off to share with you—

since I now trust your ear more than I initially trusted your voice—a couple of recent experiences in which I have felt misled and misleading. You have become my minister by being open to whatever need was embedded in my first blurted attempts to strip, or as it now seems, to test, your authority.

Of course, we got to this point more quickly in this role play than we would in most role plays and certainly more quickly than we would in most real narthex conversations, because I am accustomed to it and because I was writing your script. But the movement is real. Your honest attempt to turn the other cheek and take a good look at me, to see what else I may need if I need to take away your coat, to try to find the cadences of my stride if I seem to be forcing you off course; your earnest attempt to discover *why* I need to deliver a blow is sure to reach and touch me in some important way.

Perhaps it is not assurance that I am worried about in myself and therefore in you. Perhaps it is issues of purity and guilt. I might have said to you something like, "Maybe I am just superstitious and want to have things stay the same always, like knocking on wood." And you may reflect this anxiety with a response something like, "Because otherwise, things may go wrong." If I confirm your interpretation with a yes, you may try to touch my experience with a story from your own: "That reminds me of once when I was flying a kite with my brother. Or, rather, he was flying it and it was sailing up just fine. Then he gave me the string, and all of a sudden that kite started nose-diving and crashed into a tree. I knew what he was thinking, even though he never said it, or maybe especially because he never said it: If you let a girl touch something, she will spoil it. I guess we all have feelings like that. I have a strange thing about not wanting to get on a bus with a woman bus driver." If you share that much and that vulnerably, I may open up some more too. "As I said, it is just a superstition, probably, but it does give me a funny feeling to see a woman handling things that do need to go right." And sooner or later—perhaps later than in this quick role play—we begin to discuss the urgency, even anxiety, I feel about needing to stay in proper touch with the holy and to try to be sure that things in my life are going right, since I seem to be afflicted with some anxiety that everything may not be going right.

Grace at the Table

"If a man in authority makes you go one mile. . . ." One more role play illustrates a modern equivalent of the forced march. You be the program chairman for the school father-son banquet, and I'll be a minister you call on the phone. "We need someone to say the blessing at the meal," you say. "It's the turn this year for a Protestant, and we hope you will do it. We would like to have you come and sit at the head table, and of course we will furnish the meal. And it doesn't have to be much. In fact, the shorter the prayer the better." Your specifications are clear. But you do have one more, which is a bit awkward, "I know you don't usually wear that white clerical collar. But I wonder if you could just this once. It seems to mean something to a lot of people, especially the Catholics."

The noble traditions of the church, my own struggling to discern meaningful vocation, my long and anguished and continuing training to fit myself to fulfill that vocation, the daily discipline I impose on myself to try to be responsive to the deepest rumblings and highest aspirations of life, the careful way I budget my time to try to be a faithful steward of the little time I have available in the light of the immense needs I see —in the face of this earnestness I have about my ministry, you want me to give an evening so I can perform, like a trained dog, a short sacerdotal trick, after which you will throw me my supper and ask me to be still. I can't think of any more abrupt way of being shouldered off course.

So of course my most natural response is to resist this diversion as abruptly as it is tendered. I am committed to *ministry*, and if you want to sidetrack me into playing instant holy man according to your specifications, then I should explain, more or less politely, as to why I cannot and will not do what you want. Perhaps I can even shoulder you back onto my course. "Maybe you would like to come to our service next Sunday or to our Bible study next Wednesday, or your boy might want to come to our confirmation class." Or "I would much rather spend my time with one or two of the fathers and sons, dealing with crises they may have." Feeling insulted and demeaned, I can insult and demean in exchange, belittling as I feel belittled, making it clear that I have more important things to do than what you want. An eye-for-an-eye, and perfectly justifiable as a way of protecting my ministry, I need to define and identify my ministry in my terms by showing how yours are so far askew. Perhaps I simply shoulder you away with my busy schedule: "I really have too much to do for that sort of thing."

Then there is what may seem the opposite of the refusal, the easy compliance. "Of course I'll come. I'm flattered to be invited to do this. Yes, I can find a clerical collar. It will be fun to dress up like a priest." And my prayer is short and just the kind of ritualistic blessing of the food you want with all the cliches you expect to hear; and I make no effort in my prayer or in the table conversation to address my perception of any of the deeper issues of sex-limited groups, of family relations, or of the rather macho theme the occasion seems to assume. I come onto your turf at the high school and seem grateful to be permitted. If I feel particularly assured the next day for having been "mingling with the boys," or if I feel irritable for having abandoned my own sense of ministry and having succumbed to yours, then either is simply the price that sometimes has to be paid for "being relevant."

But neither the refusal nor the compliance takes you any

more seriously than I think your invitation takes me. In neither case do I get past the invitation and the insult or the diversion it means to me. In neither case do I try to get acquainted with you, and in neither case do I make any effort to *practice* ministry. If I refuse, I make an effort to protect or define ministry but not to practice it. If I comply, I do so knowing that I am temporarily forsaking ministry. If I am shouldered, I can shoulder back or I can let myself be carried along. But in neither case do I take deliberate steps of my own choosing and intent.

How can we role play the alternative, in which I do take steps, in which I do *practice* ministry in this situation? Let me come to the meal and let me assume, at least through the invocation, the role in which I am cast. But now that I have gone the first mile—your mile—let me go the second; during the meal let me begin the practice of ministry my way. My second mile follows in the direction set by the first, which you chose, but it's the mile I choose, and I move in it my way. Let me inquire about this undeniably urgent need for an instant holy man. I can try to do it jovially in the mood of the evening. "It cost you a $5 dinner to have me give a two-minute prayer. You don't pay that much usually for a whole Sunday church service. Is it worth it? You could say your own prayer and save the money."

What answers will you give? "Well, we are only salesmen and businessmen," one of you may say, "and what we have to sell isn't the good stuff that you know about." And so we have hints about personal misgivings about your own vocation and its worthiness or your worthiness. Or "Well, we've always had priests and ministers—and more recently, rabbis—ever since I've been coming to these things with my father, and I wouldn't want to change now." Or "This may be as close as some of these boys ever get to a minister, we ought to do at least that for them." Hints of misgivings, at least vicarious, about the way you are being fathers and looking for whatever help from the institution you can get. "Last year when it was the Catholics' turn, we had a monsignor who was very witty, and we wanted to show that we could put up someone who could match him." Rivalries and competitions hinted at.

You will say that to read these hints in these remarks is to read a lot into them, and you will be right. But it would be more wrong to close off the possibility of such hints and exploring them, for more times than not just such hints *are* signaled in these remarks and invite a gentle exploration and address. There really isn't any other way of discovering who you are and how I can minister to you except by stopping where you are and looking and listening. There doesn't seem to be any better occasion for practicing ministry than when you are already taking me and my ministry, at least your perception of it, seriously enough to encounter me, even when the encounter feels like a blow. You are on your path of searching for ministry, and I am on my path pursuing ministry. When these paths cross, the crossing may be abrupt and painful. But the crossing is the point where we may, together, discover a ministry graciously different from either of our set paths—if at least one of us can turn and look at the other.

5. Seeing through Expectations to Find Ministry

One day at three in the afternoon, the hour of prayer, Peter and John were on their way up to the temple. Now a man who had been a cripple from birth used to be carried there and laid every day by the gate of the temple called "Beautiful Gate," to beg from people as they went in. When he saw Peter and John on their way into the temple he asked for alms. But Peter fixed his eyes on him, as John did also, and said, "Look at us." Expecting a gift from them, the man was all attention to Peter. And Peter said, "I have no silver or gold; but what I have I give you: in the name of Jesus Christ of Nazareth, walk." Then he grasped him by the right hand and pulled him up; and at once his feet and ankles grew strong; he sprang up, stood on his feet, and started to walk. He entered the temple with them, leaping and praising God as he went. Everyone saw him walking and praising God, and when they recognized him as a man who used to sit begging at Beautiful Gate, they were filled with wonder and amazement at what had happened to him.

Acts 3:1–10

The first recorded moment of pastoral ministry in the Christian church is a moment of intense mutual frustration and a moment of joyful mutual discovery, in that frustration, of fulfilling ministry.

Mutual frustration: The ministers and the beggar said no to

Portions of this chapter originally appeared in James E. Dittes, "Who Calls Us 'Healer'?" *The Christian Ministry* (July 1972), pp. 6–14, copyright © The Christian Century Foundation, 1972. Reprinted by permission.

each other. Peter and John were practicing their ministry; as was their habit, they were going to the temple to pray and were recruiting others to join them. The man declined to join them; he said no to their ministry. As was his habit, he demanded ministry in different terms, alms. They said no to that; they declined to practice ministry as he had defined it. Ministers and beggar could each feel stranded, abandoned by the other.

Mutual discovery: The apostles and the beggar took each other's no seriously. The apostles abandoned (temporarily) their path to prayer. The beggar abandoned his plea for alms. They gave up their *habits* of ministry, which failed to reach each other, and discovered that within those habits were *intentions* of ministry—for wholeness and health—that did converge. They gave up their habituated forms of ministry, and in the space thus opened they found new forms. The no-saying made them deviate from "ministry"; the deviation allowed them to find ministry. The no-saying, taken seriously, made their ministry more not less—more faithful and true not less, more fulfilling of intentions not less. By the Beautiful Gate, in the openness left by abandoned prayer and denied alms, ministers and beggar discovered healing and celebrated together.

The no-saying presupposed a yes-saying. Apostles and beggar were committed to ministry but to differing and contradictory *habits* of ministry. So it is with the usual impasse between minister and people. They are both committed to ministry, genuinely committed. And they express that commitment in entrenched, habituated forms of ministry. Indeed, the earnestness of their commitment is expressed in the firmness of their habits. People less committed to ministry would be less likely to confront each other, to say no to each other, with their contradictory habits, and also less likely to feel so anguished when they *heard* a no.

In their habits the minister says, "I see ministry this way," and the people say, "No, we see ministry another way." The minister says, "I see our need and God's intended presence in our need this way." The people say, "No, we don't see our need or God's response that way. We see our need differently and we recognize the role of God and church and ministry in our lives in quite different ways." The minister instructs the pulpit committee and the deacons and the congregation in how to be a minister of God and a church of God. And the people instruct the minister. Peter and John said, "Join us in prayer." The man at the gate said, "No, I'm not coming in; instead, give me alms." The apostles were determined in their particular new habit of ministry by the intensity of their recent experience (at Pentecost). The man was determined in his particular habit of ministry by lifelong practice. So with most ministers and people: The intensity of recent experience (as at seminary) and the entrenchment of lifelong practice firm and confirm the conflicting habits of ministry.

The minister says, "What you need and what I must do is to deepen the liturgical meaning of our worship." The people say, "No, what we need is to sing our familiar hymns; to be our minister, you must learn and lead and like them."

A man may say, "Get me a job. You know people in town and they'll listen to you, if you'll only try to help me." "No," a minister may reply. "I am here to help you get Christ. Seek first the kingdom of heaven, and these things will be added unto you."

The minister says, "You need to take God's word (and my ministry) more seriously in your lives, as with committed Bible study, or discussion of the sermon after church." The people say, "What we need is for *you* to *tell* us of God's word and for us to gather and chat after church on the front steps or over coffee."

The people say, "We need the impact in our lives that comes from having the minister call in our homes regularly, even though briefly." The minister says, "No, I can have impact where it is needed in your lives by being available regularly in my office for counseling you through crises."

The minister says, "What this community needs, and the response God wants us to make, is to develop a halfway house for ex-prisoners." The people say, "No, *our* community responsibility more naturally takes the form of providing space for Alcoholics Anonymous, Boy Scouts, and overflow classes from the high school."

The people say, "Can't you get my husband to stop drinking?" or "Please try to get my kids to understand how much they are hurting themselves with that junk!" The minister says, "No, I can't do that until they ask me. Tell me *your* problems."

A minister says, "We should spend at least $100 of our church scholarship money to offer a camp tuition for a kid from the inner city." A trustee says, "Tell me one good reason why we should."

The minister says, "Since you call me to be your minister, join me in these things. How can I be a minister—as I feel deeply called to be—if you will not be a church by taking your part in responding to God's call in worship and in word, in personal and community crises?" The people say, "No, how can we be a church—as we deeply and traditionally feel called to be—if you will not be our minister by taking your role in these activities?"

Such encounters are what sociologists call role conflict, what journalists call the crunch or the gathering storm, what ministers and people call impossible as they leave ministry and the church—by different doors or gates. Minister and people stay with their habits of ministry and turn away from each other, and thereby from ministry.

But by the Beautiful Gate the apostles and the beggar did not turn away from each other or from the frustrations of their encounter or from the possibilities for ministry opened by those frustrations. Each did, decidedly, turn away from their habits of ministry, their perfectly valid entrenched expectations that ministry was to be found in the sharing of prayer or in the giving of alms. But they did not turn away from the visions and yearnings lodged in those expectations. Their reaching out in prayer and in alms asking was animated by yearnings for wholeness of life and for sharing of life. They held fast to these yearnings even while they abandoned the ministry they had supposed embodied them. The apostles yearned for all to be touched in their brokenness with the vibrant, surprising, life-giving, and faithful power of the spirit of God they had just encountered at Pentecost. So they looked for and invited others to look for this spirit in the gathering at prayers, where they had encountered it. The cripple yearned for remedy and for greater wholeness and looked for it (and invited others to contribute to it) in the only way he knew, alms. But then each surrendered these habituated patterns of ministry, which did not touch each other, and thereby opened the way for their yearnings to emerge and to be joined by the spirit in a new moment and act of ministry.

Interrupting the route to prayer and denying the demands for alms, Peter took the cripple by the hand. In that sudden touching of yearnings each risked an unfamiliar and unlikely act of ministry. In sacrificing their habituated expectations of ministry, they found, together—it could not have been otherwise than together, it could not have been otherwise than in sacrifice of expectations—a surprising meeting of their yearnings in a new wholeness.

This encounter of apostles and cripple at the Beautiful Gate teaches of the call to ministry that is in the shattering of habits of ministry. This encounter at the Beautiful Gate teaches also of the call to ministry that is in the discernment of yearnings *within* the fixed habits of ministry, yearnings revealed more easily by the shattering of those patterns.

Peter and John were not just summoners to prayer and not

just deniers of alms, and the cripple was not just an abstainer from prayer and a demander of alms—although the no-saying is often all that ministers and people can hear in each other. The apostles were yearners after the wholeness of life that is nourished by living it with God. Such yearning, though obvious, is readily obscured in our times by battles over patterns of ministry. The man by the gate was a cripple, in need of God's wholeness, and presumably—long buried by habituation to his lameness and to alms—a yearner for the wholeness. *This* yearning, though obvious, is also readily obscured by battles over patterns of ministry.

The apostles and the beggar said no to each other. They found ministry by taking the no very seriously and listening to the positive summons lodged in the no. The apostles took the beggar's no seriously in two ways: First, they accepted it as a no to them. If he could not go with them in their patterns of ministry, if these did not meet his needs, they could give up (at least temporarily) their patterns of ministry and stay with him, in search of new ministry. This was genuine sacrifice and risky venture. That's what the no meant to *them:* a frustration of intentions and a call to sacrifice. They accepted this. Second, they were attuned to what the no meant to the beggar, to what it meant beyond merely no. It meant other needs were clamoring for attention and ministry, yearnings that found expression, blunt and blunted to be sure, in the no. They also found expression, still blunt and blunted, in the demand for alms. But the apostles could also take seriously their own no to the alms. Their no was a way of looking into not a way of looking away from. To take seriously the no was to unpeel the definitions, the roles, the patterns of ministry that evoked them, and thus to open the yearnings within those patterns to greater self-consciousness and to each other. "I have no silver and gold; but what I have I give you." No to the gold is a means of discerning more clearly "what I have." No to the gold is a means of discerning more clearly the "you." The no is a prelude to matching these—"what I have" and "you"—in a new moment of ministry.

"Peter fixed his eyes on him. . . ."

When Peter looked at the man, what did he see? He saw a beggar, yes. He also saw a cripple. He also saw a whole man. To fix his eyes on *him*, to see him wholly, to minister to him, Peter needed to see all three.

It is too easy for the minister to see only the beggar, the one who is defining what the minister should do—in this case, give alms. "Expecting a gift from them, the man was all attention." It is easy to be lured into the roles that people would define and to call that ministry; the minister may call it "relevance," and critical onlookers may say "sell-out." "I have no silver or gold. . . ." It is easy to deny the roles that people would define and to call *that* ministry; the minister may speak of "transcendent higher callings," and the critical onlooker may say "cop-out." Peter and John could have seen only the beggar; they could have dropped in their coins, dutifully and with satisfaction, and gone on their way, never really noticing his real needs or possibilities, that he was also a cripple and also a whole man. Or they could have overlooked his begging, urging him to come to prayer and feeling satisfaction from *that;* again not noticing his needs or possibilities, not seeing that he was a cripple or a whole man, which were signaled by his begging.

When vocational identity—call—is uncertain or under challenge, then it is especially tempting to don the role expectations of others, especially when these are as firmly entrenched in habit and culture as alms giving, making moral and biblical pronouncements, saying grace at women's fellowship and Kiwanis luncheons, or supporting gospel hymns and Boy Scouts.

Whether we comply or defy, if all we can see is the expectation, then we cannot see the needs and the possibilities it points to.

The minister needs to see but also to see through the expectations others have for ministry. Peter and John could see the man as cripple and as whole man precisely because they could see him as beggar. "Peter fixed his eyes on him." Peter could recognize and accept him so unambiguously as beggar that he could see through the begging and see him whole. The apostles could see the man's expectations for ministry so clearly that they could say no to those expectations and minister to him.

There were bystanders by the Beautiful Gate. Alms giving is what they all expected, and when the apostles insisted on seeing through the alms asking and alms giving to recognize and respond to the needs signaled by the alms asking—to see the man as cripple and as whole—they offended the crowds and precipitated stormy dispute with the authorities. Ministry lies precisely in seeing through the facades, in exposing and exploring and changing questions more than in giving answers, in enlarging quest and demand more than in fulfilling settled and conventional role expectations. Ministry is in seeing through what others see as a matter of course, what others accept blindly, and this is never more true than with the expectations of ministry that others hold routinely. These expectations are tempting, for they do provide models of ministry and they are well entrenched and acceptable in church and culture. Alms giving would have done *something* for the man, and it was what everybody expected. But these expectations are challenging and need to be challenged just because they are others' expectations, the world's expectations, the devices worked out by the world to heal itself, the devices that therefore perpetuate the brokenness as much as heal it. The giving of alms, what everyone expects, measures and continues the crippledness not heals it. Alms demean the man, confirm him in his lameness, and in fact become the very measure of the distance between his state and health. Peter and John, refusing to measure out with alms this distance between him and them, the distance between brokenness and wholeness, saw the man as already participating with them in a world of vigor and wholeness. They insisted on proclaiming what they saw, by joyful deed and joyful word, together.

But the minister who ventures to live and to proclaim this more penetrating vision of wholeness represents a world alien to the broken world that is calling for ministry. That alienation is precisely why one ministers, but it is also precisely what ruptures ministry, the rupture of trying to represent wholeness to a world of brokenness. The world of brokenness confronts ministry not only with its ills but also with the prescriptions and remedies it has tried to devise for its ills, prescriptions and remedies that represent the brokenness and confirm it.

Society as a whole, not just needy individuals at the temple gate or the church assembled within, extends its hand and its definition of temptingly precise and gratifyingly recognized forms of ministry. Recognizable and recognized healers in our culture are physicians, psychiatrists, social workers, psychologists, sensitivity trainers, maybe in special ways people like city planners and teachers—all members of established professions, as established as responses to disease in our culture as alms giving was in another. It is natural for a minister to try to find call, established vocational identity, by alliance with or imitation of one of these professions. But these professions, and the very notion of professionalization, are ways that the world has devised to respond to its own ills, and, as a consequence, they participate in and perpetuate the ills as much as they mitigate them. The very professional status that provides the minister with the secure role definition preserves the "client's" role definition of insecurity. The exalted status of the professional enhances the client's sense of alienation and separation from healing and from agents of healing. The same professionalization that accords the minister new identity imprisons the clients with newly circumscribed and prescribed definitions of *their* situation. They become "patients" or "clients" and assume those "problems" the social worker or psychological counselor or ministerial imitator is prepared to solve. They are to that degree closed off from a more complete understanding of their situation. When seen only as beggars, they see themselves only as beggars. In aspiring to and accepting the professional status that society affords, the minister participates in and perpetuates a depersonalization that is one of the principal ills of society and of those he or she would heal.

The giving of alms measures rather than heals the illness.

We are called to be ministers by the intentions of God for his broken world. He intends his people to be whole, and he is at work to make us whole. Because we are his, we, too, work toward wholeness for all. But because we are also broken members of an alienated world, God's call is not enough for us. The world and our inner brokenness compel us to identify our ministry and to measure it, and the terms we borrow from the world to measure by are the tasks of doing well and doing good. When we are at the task of enabling others to do good (by coaching them with pronouncements of the good and the good ways to achieve it) and when we are at the task of enabling others to do well (coaching and goading them to successful performance of prescribed social roles), then we are doing well, and in that we can claim a professional role, one recognized by the world and therefore by us. So our calling to be ministers of God becomes embodied in the professional role definitions of the world, as these are lodged in us and as they are lodged in all those about us who give them compelling voice. We use the world's acclaim for good works to identify

and justify ourself. To establish our own vocation, we contort
our true vocation: the call to be one of God's people.

Yet ministry must remain in the world, even though not of
it, especially ministry in the name of the Incarnate Lord. So
Christian ministry proceeds by a kind of stumbling, crunching
rhythm, accommodating itself to the terms of the culture and
the world it would yet transform ("I have become all things to
all men, that I might by all means save some," 1 Cor. 9:22, rsv)
yet stoutly resisting—by seeing through—the terms of the
world it would nevertheless move easily among ("Do not be
conformed to this world, but be transformed by the renewal
of your mind . . ." Rom. 12:2, rsv).

"Get me a job. You know people in town and they'll listen to
you, if you'll only try to help me."

In this demand and definition of ministry, the minister may
see a chance to be effective in a way that can be measured by
the helped individual and acclaimed by the community. "Now
you are showing that ministers can really do something use-
ful." So the minister may scurry off to find the job and feel
gratified at this "new form of ministry in a secular age."

Or the demand may be seen as pure distraction from ministry. The minister may summarily dismiss or refer the request
or even locate a job, so as quickly to get back to the preaching
or Bible study or prayer or whatever is construed as true ministry, letting it proceed untouching and untouched by the demand for the job.

Or it is possible to fix our eyes, to look so closely and
carefully at the demand for the job as to take it seriously and
to see through it, to see what needs and possibilities for ministry are signaled by this demand. The demand for help in
finding a job *is* more likely a symptom of brokenness than it
is a prescription for remedy. To help find the job feeds that
symptom more than it heals. Alms giving confirms the lame-

ness. For a man to come to the minister and ask for this help in finding a job is to afford the minister a good glimpse of what is wrong not of how it can be made right.

If there are jobs to be had for the minister's asking (a genuine shortage of jobs would be a different case), then presumably there are also jobs for the man's asking. His plea for help becomes a measure of . . . what? Maybe his own sense of inadequacy, maybe his desperate fears of facing risks, maybe rigid defense against facing any realistic self-appraisal, maybe avoidance of other distresses by insisting that the job is the problem, maybe other revealingly idolatrous addiction to work, maybe a desire to capture the minister (and God?) to his bidding. We don't know until we get past his definition of ministry. ("I have no silver and gold.") Or more accurately, we won't know what his definition for our ministry means to him until we get past what it means to us.

But we can be reasonably sure that in his demands are more clues to his ailing than to his healing, clues to the difficulties he had in holding a job and undoubtedly to other distresses in his life. These clues can become occasions of healing ministry. But so long as we accept his definition of ministry, offer the alms he asks, and move on, we can never help him perceive or experience the world in which he could walk—no matter how much genuine gratitude he may feel for generous alms and how much acclaim bystanders may shower on us.

"Can't you get my husband to stop drinking?" "Please try to get my kids to understand how much they are hurting themselves with that junk!"

Drug abuse, by whatever generation, is a real problem; and when the abuser asks for help, that will be one occasion for important ministry. When the wife or father asks the minister to shape up another person, that is something else. The alms they ask may help. The minister may scurry off on the assigned mission to reform the husband or the kids, and any partial success or even the effort will certainly win community acclaim and fervent personal gratitude. But it will not heal the lameness or hear the yearning in the asking.

The minister may, quite accurately, recognize that effective ministry to the abuser cannot begin with spouses' or parents' wishes and therefore summarily dismiss the request: "No, I can't do that until they ask me. But I will listen while you tell me *your* problems." But this will not heal the lameness or hear the yearning in the asking either.

What lameness may be seen in and through the asking? Anger at abandonment? Fear of censure, public or self-administered, for failure as wife or father? Fear of joining in such self-indulgence? Maybe some of the same impatience with deviation or intolerance of others' distress that has contributed to husband's or child's abuse? Turning to the minister is part of the larger brokenness of the family, of which the drug abuse is also part, just as alms asking is part of what defines the cripple. And we can call the cripple to health only when we see the crippledness in the alms asking as much as in the lame legs. Then we can move beyond, to ministry of healing.

"Tell me one good reason why we should spend at least $100 of our church scholarship money to offer a camp tuition for a kid from the inner city." Here the definition of ministry—"Tell me one good reason"—is less dramatic than the demand for a job or for moral reform of relatives and is obscured by the controversy over the budget item. Nevertheless, the minister, in this case, is being instructed in how to play her role in that controversy: supply reasons. This is one of the most conventional roles—making pronouncements—into which ministers are assigned. The minister is more than ready to comply, predisposed by all the other expectations—of the liberals on the Christian education committee, of the seminary professors, of her husband, of all those who would charter and acclaim ministry in the form of "giving reasons." Win or lose the $100 budget item, win or lose the trustee, a vigorous ministry of giving stalwart reasons will be admired and gratifying. It also will not address whatever special possibilities for ministry are lodged in this form of this request.

Or the request for reasons may be simply recognized as the distraction and the obstacle that it is, in the way of the modest plan for the church to contribute to an individual from the inner city. "Let's talk about that later." "Let's get on with the rest of the budget and the vote." "I intend to preach about this next month." "I'll give you an article I read that may help." Defying the demand may also be gratifying to the minister and to onlookers, but it, like complying, does not address whatever possibilities for ministry may be lodged in this form of this request.

The request, trivial and distracting as it may seem, can nevertheless be seen through to ministry. It can be recognized as a symptom. Such reasoning and debating partakes more of the devisiveness than of the wholeness of the community and the individuals within it. It partakes more of the preoccupation and protection of self and of "mine" than of sharing life with others. It participates more in the justification of self than in the humiliation of self. It must be that the same constriction of outlook that prompted fear of spending $100 "outside" also prompts the form of the question ("Can we justify this?"). To respond to the question in its terms, to supply the arguments, to make one faction of the church prevail over another faction —this mode of behavior confirms and feeds the constricted outlook it would profess to undo.

There are other ways of identifying and responding to the apprehensions and constrictions present in the trustee's demands. But they all presuppose resisting his definition, and probably also the Christian education committee's definition, of the minister's task at the time. And they all presuppose the minister's ability to transcend the confining terms of the meeting and to see the trustee as one who can walk forth upright as an adult among other adults despite his present cowering behind a narrow demand for narrow ministry. The minister can find ways to say, "Let's talk about this later" that seem to take the request, and the trustee, seriously not dismiss it and him. The minister can cut through the petty debate and say, wholeheartedly and warmly, as in this case she did, "Oh, we are too good friends to have to pretend that we are in a debating society or a courtroom. You've been a tightwad for twenty years with the church's money; we all know that and thank you for it. We wouldn't be where we are today if you weren't. But we also know you have a lot of trouble, more than you want even, seeing what's important about relating to the people in the inner city. Maybe you always will, but I hope not. And I think maybe you hope not, too. Let's not take time for 'reasons' now. Maybe you will or won't approve this $100 item. But let's save the time and I'll take you out to camp next month and make you meet the kid."

"Look at us. . . . What I have I give you"

But all of this is only half of what is to be learned about ministry at the Beautiful Gate. This has been about people's expectations for the minister and how they can be broken open and seen through, frustrated even while taken seriously, so as to find space and focus for ministry. The alms giving was recognized and denied so that the cripple and the whole man could be recognized. But the apostles, too, had expectations that had to be broken open and seen through so that the yearnings and intentions within *those* expectations could be released and meet the man's. "Peter fixed his eyes on him." Peter turned aside from his course for prayer, wholeheartedly turned aside and *fixed* his attention on the *man*. He abandoned, for the time being, his appointment for prayer but not his mood of joyful faith in God's gracious power, which the prayer was to express. Indeed, he abandoned his appointment for prayer so as to unlock and disclose just that joyful faith in God's gracious power. It became more abundant and available in the breaking of the appointment than it would have been in its keeping. The minister's expectations no less than the man's had to be broken open and seen through so that the yearnings in each could meet in ministry.

Long-time, entrenched, established habits and patterns and appointments of ministry, which a minister brings to any situation, are no less tempting and no less challenging and no less in need of challenge than are the demands people seem to impose on the minister. They are no less symptoms of brokenness, nor are they any less signals of possibility, vessels of promise. The minister's expectations are bolstered, too, often from the past. Going to the temple to pray, like alms giving, was what everybody expected and approved. So with helping people to "get Christ . . . to seek first the kingdom of heaven" (even when opposed to helping people get jobs) or with talking to people about their own problems or with pushing through a $100 tuition. So, too, with developing halfway houses and with reserving time for crisis counseling and with renewal of the worship service. But all of these perfectly legitimate calls need to be set aside on occasion, on the occasion when they run athwart conflicting demands that would call forth from these calls the Call they signal. But it is especially when call—vocational identity—is uncertain or under challenge, especially in these occasions of thwarting, that a minister clings most tenaciously and desperately to those forms of calls that give expression to, even as they obscure, the fundamental yearnings and commitments of his or her ministry.

"We should spend at least $100 of our church scholarship money to offer a camp tuition for a kid from the inner city." The minister's proposal expresses well a fundamental commitment and yearning for wholeness among God's people. The proposal is all the trustee can see, just as alms asking is all some ministers can see. Can the minister behave in such a way that the trustee can "see through" the proposal and experience the yearning for wholeness within it? She can, as many ministers do, stick firmly to the proposal as the best way of expressing that commitment and yearning, and thereby prevent the trustee from discerning and experiencing it. Or she can abandon the proposal, either under fire or so as to return the fire, and thereby again prevent the trustee from discerning and experiencing the commitment to wholeness the proposal signals. Or she can hold to the proposal but loosely enough so as to leave room for the trustee to see more than just the proposal and for her to express her commitment for wholeness of community. This is what she seems to have done in the rejoinder quoted above. She was ready to forsake for a time her own proposal, just as she was ready to forsake for a time the trustee's demands for reasons. And in the room left by that forsaking, the minister was able to bespeak and enact more wholeness, in the trustee, in the trustee's meeting, and between the trustee and the inner-city kid, than she could have by insisting on the proposal to which she had, thirty minutes earlier, been insistently committed as a crucial expression of wholeness. So it is a *mutual* frustration of expectations—the "Me, too" readiness of the minister to be off balance and vulnerable, deprived of the comfort and security of conventional roles, that permits ministry. If the minister can let go and open up, then perhaps the people can, too. But the mutualness is more focused than that. Since they share the moment of confrontation, they share a lot. If habitual expectations of ministry are colliding, then the commitments and yearnings embodied in those expectations are in touch, and at some point they must converge.

The minister says, "What you need and what I must do is to deepen the liturgical meaning of our worship." The people say, "No, what we need is to sing our familiar hymns." It looks like a classic impasse, minister and people saying a resolute no to each other's patterns and expectations of worship. But only the slightest effort is needed to see through these conflicting expectations and discern the converging and mutual yearnings and intentions within them. Both are seeking genuine and meaningful religious experience. The more formal liturgy has been meaningful for the minister, has made touch with the resources of community and heritage and symbol, has made God more vividly and vitally present. The familiar hymns have put the people in touch with the resources of community and heritage and symbol that make God more vitally and vividly present to them. Both want to reconfirm and enhance the memory of genuine religious experience, one through the continuities of a sung Psalm, the other through the continuities of "The Old Rugged Cross."

When they say no to each other's preferences, it seems at first as though they are saying no to the yearnings. It can be, and usually is, a time of hurt and frustration and battle and rupture of ministry. But if they can—it is the minister's role to lead this heeding—fix their eyes firmly on each other, take each other's expectations seriously enough to see through them and to discover the common yearning, then the confrontation becomes a time of blended ministry: Although your ways are not my ways, and my ways are not your ways, we want the same things.

In one church just such a moment of impasse yielded a startling new sense of community, some fresh symbols, and a striking feeling of the creative and redemptive power of God.

...in good humor and trust the minister and the people said to each other: "Look, when you come right down to it for us, in this suburb, nearing the twenty-first century, there are forms potentially richer than either a chanted Psalm or the 'Old Rugged Cross.'" They even disbanded the choir, and those who had needed the choir now found some of their needs better met in the team that every Thursday evening (formerly choir practice night) planned the coming week's worship, and some other needs met in introducing and explaining the Sunday worship to their congregation each week. The church happened to turn mostly to guitar music, some on records and some live, and to other forms that may prove to have had even a shorter life span than chanted Psalms and evangelical hymns. But the church will be ready when the time comes again to say no.

Meanwhile, the sharing of the no and the impetus it gave to new community and newly meaningful worship was symbolized, crudely but most intimately, in a moment the committee included in the morning worship about once a month: The minister started to chant a Psalm, which was the cue for the congregation to begin singing "Let the Lower Lights Be Burning." And the counterpoint resolved, after "You May Rescue You May Save," into a joyful singing of "Amazing Grace," which for this congregation was a fresh and striking hymn. The ritual was a bit corny but genuine, and it always evoked spirited participation, much turning of heads, and exchanging of smiles. It was indeed effective celebration of the real life this community discovered when expectations of worship were disrupting and disrupted to make room for new experiences of worship that made God more vividly and vitally present.

The apostles, deterred from their prayers, refusing alms, took the hand of the man and said, "In the name of Jesus Christ of Nazareth, walk."

"Intense crisis counseling," the minister says; and the people say, "No, regular brief home visits." The scene is the last regular deacon's meeting of the year, this minister's first year in the church, and the minister is making a report of his pastoral work. He wants the deacons to know that he is now spending between five and ten hours a week in intense pastoral counseling with members of the church, and two or three hours a week with nonmembers. People stop in his office, by appointment, for an hour or an hour and a half, usually every week or every two weeks. He wants to tell the deacons this because they probably wouldn't know it otherwise—this part of ministry is quiet and confidential—and because it is something of considerable satisfaction, even pride, for the minister. He has invested much training and experience; he goes to an annual summer workshop in psychological and psychiatrically oriented training for clergy. He is persuaded that it is crucial for clergy to be able to offer this professional expertise and is delighted that even in his first year he has developed the reputation and trust that nourish this kind of counseling ministry.

But the minister's enthusiasm is hardly echoed by the deacons. There are a couple of polite "That's interesting" remarks, and one deacon asks, with genuine uncertainty and curiosity not with hostility or humor, "You just sit and talk like we are doing, or do you use a couch or something?" They see —or fail to see—this intense counseling only at face value (as the apostles might have seen the man at the gate only as an alms asker, or the man might have seen the apostles only as prayer-bound). And the minister *could* see this coolness, at face value, as resistance to this important ministry.

But the minister is willing and able to invite them to fix their eyes on each other and see through this initial face-off. He looks squarely at their subtle no-saying and invites them to do likewise, so as to open it up and understand what it encodes. "I don't exactly see you all lining up at my door, and maybe you are wondering why anybody does." The minister speaks with the same directness yet openness that has earned him the trust and developed the counseling ministry he has just been speaking of. And the deacons respond in the same way as those who have come for counseling: "Well, that probably doesn't leave you time for other things, or for other people at least." "I guess we are a little more used to ministers who come out to see us rather than ask us to come see them." "This would really be good, for you to tell everybody how much of this you do. When we don't see you in our homes very much, we can easily forget that you *are* seeing some of us." The minister is hearing a familiar complaint and expectation: Call in our homes regularly, like ministers always have, or you aren't really being our minister.

But instead of seeing these complaints only as complaints, which might make him either defensive or compliant, he tries to fix his eyes—and the deacons'—firmly on the complaints, so as to see through them. "I hear you loud and clear. You miss it, or think some of the people miss it, that I don't get out into the homes more often and more regularly."

"Well, there's something special about having the minister in the house, even if he doesn't stay there long." Or "One of my earliest memories is having the minister stop in for tea when I was a little boy. That always seemed to make supper special after that, and he always had a nice word for me too." Or "Some things shouldn't change, even when everything else does, or maybe especially when everything else does." Or "We all need some attention, not just the squeaky hinges. Sometimes it just doesn't feel right to call up and make an appointment to see your minister, like he was a doctor or someone; that's like making an appointment to see your wife." Soon the deacons are talking, relatively comfortably, about some of the concerns that were encoded in their coolness to the idea of intensive crisis counseling for the few. A sociologist who was listening might speak about alienation, about the anxiety over loss of stable and intimate and familiar ties to significant people and to significant values. The ebbing quality of their life seems symbolized and worsened by the apparently increasing professional remoteness of the minister. The minister they need is a member of the family, a very special member of the family, not a skilled professional.

The minister gives ear and gives voice, a discerning and a compassionate voice, to these complaints-become-confessions, in a way that is both like a member of the family and like a skilled professional.

But that is not all the minister does. He remembers that it is his own strong commitment—perhaps, one might even say, addiction—to formal and intensive and personal counseling that has started the conversation. It is not fair or ministerial, although perhaps it is "professional," to turn the analysis only on the deacons. If there is a second mile to go, one ought to go *with* them. So he offers his own "Me, too" confession. He invites all to fix their eyes on him and help him see through his own strong habits of ministry.

The minister gradually comes to realize and to share such self-recognition as this: "I know what you are talking about when you talk about the 'specialness' of having the minister in your house, and also when you talk about how hard it seems to be these days to get really close to people that you want to get close to, and also when you talk about feeling left out, as when you feel the minister is slighting some members of the parish for a kind of elite corps of counselees. I feel that same kind of need for specialness, especially in personal relations, and I guess that's one thing that makes me comfortable with intense and prolonged personal counseling. We do get down to special things, and we do get close to each other in ways that don't seem to happen so much when I stop in the house for coffee or whatever. It may be true that I am looking for some of the same things in this counseling ministry that you are looking for when you ask me to call in your homes. I also know what it means to feel left out, I think, because any new minister coming into a settled congregation feels kind of an outsider, and as often as I may call in your homes, this still doesn't go away too easily. So I suspect that I cast around for my own special circle of people I can feel more easily that I belong with, and I suppose that's one thing I get out of these more intimate and more intense counseling relationships. This is a confession; it shouldn't be that way, but I am just telling you that I think I can understand, in my own way, what you are talking about."

Some of the deacons seem taken aback by this fixing of eyes and seeing through; they are more accustomed to and feel more comfortable with leaving things at face value and arguing, politely, about church policies and calling schedules and the like. But most deacons are energetically and unself-consciously involved, on the edges of their chairs, experiencing a rare moment of intimacy and sharing an honest openness. Suddenly, one blurts out, "We are talking about sharing and about specialness and about getting together—and here we are doing it!" Before long, they are making commitments, which they mean and mostly are able to keep, to have a discussion like this at every deacons' meeting in the coming year about what they decide to call, straightforwardly, "what the church really means to me." In the course of the following year there is less formal intensive office counseling than in the preceeding year and much less restless demand for visiting in the home. Instead, there is more of the ministry that each was pointing to.

Can there be a sense of ministry and of healing that is freed of the futile and self-defeating scramble for defined roles and yet is still credible? Can a minister truly abandon the search for defined status, articulated identity, professional roles and, by the terms of such criteria as these, be nothing and still be minister? Indeed, can one be a minister just because he or she is "nothing?" Is there any recognizable roleless role, identity-less identity? Or must such talk be limited to ordination rhetoric—ministry of faith and not of self-justifying good works, commitments and calling that transcend the social- and self-reward system that sanctions roles and professionalization, healing gospel ministry of joyful self-abandon. Is there really a style or mood of ministry that forsakes roles and in that forsaking becomes ministry?

If we contemplate such a style of self-abandonment in ministry, a ministry without role definition, do we feel this to be a weakness and an emptiness, an unjustified status, as it seems in the eyes of the world? ("What *do* you ministers do to earn your money?") Or can we credibly claim such a style as a positive, vigorous selfhood and ministry of a new order, perhaps of a new age? Can it be such even though the world (and therefore many of us much of the time) cannot recognize it?

"But whoever loses his life for my sake, he will save it." Mightily as we struggle to define ourselves, establish ourselves, justify ourselves with our measured and measurable doings, we only succeed in establishing our brokenness. Our role as minister does not come into being by our efforts to minister. If our being is not to be found up the stepped path of our doings, dare we seek it down the steep, risky path of nonbeing?

6. Lost Sheep at Grace Church Day-Care Center

"This fellow," they said, "welcomes sinners and eats with them."
He answered them with this parable: "If one of you has a hundred
sheep and loses one of them, does he not leave the ninety-nine in the
open pasture and go after the missing one until he has found it?
How delighted he is then! He lifts it on to his shoulders and home
he goes to call his friends and neighbors together. 'Rejoice with me!'
he cries. 'I have found my lost sheep!' "

Luke 15:2–6

"Be the good shepherd!" is what ministers most often hear
and tell others to hear in the parable of the lost sheep. "Be
gentle and strong. Above all, able! *Find* the lost sheep and
bring them home, in triumph and to plaudits." "Yes, yes," I
answer. "I want to be like the compassionate and virile good
shepherd, like Jesus. We all do. Others are weak and loveless,
and I must be strong and loving and help them." So the good
news of the gospel becomes a burden, the vision of *God's*
Kingdom becomes a blueprint for *my* labors, a criterion for my
accomplishments. What is offered to me as a free gift becomes
a task I must perform. My anxieties to guarantee my own place
in the Kingdom compel me to make that place as host (which
always compels me to make others be guests) rather than to
believe that I am welcome as guest.

But the parable contains another message, probably the one
Jesus intended: "You have a good shepherd." When you are
lost, you will be found; alone, you will be joined; cast down,

you will be lifted up; loveless, loved. Even you (even if you are
a minister, even if you are an established member of an established church) may be weak and wandering, aimless and inept,
without forfeiting your place in the Kingdom. Indeed, when
you are lost, let it be just so. There, too—no, there especially
—is God's love and ministry. Thanks be to God.

This chapter tells of two "Lost Sheep" sermons preached a
year apart by one minister, Tom Goddard, and of the moment
of ministry in the life of his parish, Grace Church, during that
year. In the first sermon others outside the church were the
lost sheep, their "lostness" defined in terms of their differences from members of the congregation, and the church people were urged to join the minister in being good shepherds
—caring and searching, finding and saving. In the second sermon, Tom Goddard spoke more simply, out of his own experience, of how it feels to be lost and of how it feels to be found.
Though he spoke mostly from his own experience, the congregation heard him as speaking about their experiences; though
he spoke mostly about his own yearnings, they heard echoes
of their yearning to be found and to be returned to the flock
and the open spaces. He celebrated the discovery that minister
and church people could find themselves lost and still be
found, that God says yes even when the people can't—even
when the people say no.

They had become lost in trying so hard to be good shepherds; undoubtedly, they had tried so hard to be good shepherds in the first place to quell their feelings of lostness. The
minister and the people needed to find a place as a good
shepherd—the message of the first sermon—just because they
felt unsure of any place. So when they faltered in their mission
to be good shepherds, they felt all the more lost. But then—
the message of the second sermon—their lostness compelled
and allowed them to be found, to find themselves, and—grace-
ful irony—to find those (other) lost sheep they had sought.

As long as the minister or church people looked for others by looking *down*, from the coveted posture of stalwart shepherd, they could neither find the others nor find themselves as the shepherds they needed to be. When minister or people conceded themselves also lost in the thickets and ravines and looked *up*, to be found, they could also look *nearby* and discover the others. In the floundering of the project he and they had devised for reaching out to others, they found themselves reached to and reaching others in surprising, genuine, and saving ministry.

Here are synopses of the two sermons.

The First Lost Sheep Sermon

There are a lot of lost sheep out there. We huddle together here in the comfortable life, the "open pasture," and ignore the ones who are separated from the kind of life we know. They often have different colored skin or different religious background, or speak English with an accent; they don't have the educational and economic and church advantages we have. Finding themselves lost in the thickets means living in crowded conditions, not being able to get well-paying jobs, maybe no jobs, so their family lives are disrupted, and sometimes they are even hungry and cold—literally shivering lost sheep. Sometimes, in their desperation, in their lostness, they thrash about, as lost animals may, and lurch this way and that; so we see drugs, violence, loose sex, broken families; and we need to understand this as part of their lostness, maybe as part of their cries for help. We need to find ways to bring them back, with rejoicing, to the main flock, the main paths, where they belong. We who *have*, have with our privileges also our responsibilities; we dare not be comfortable in our "open pasture" without hearing the cries of the lost and setting out to bring them back; we must use our advantages to help those with less.

Why don't people, such as members of this congregation, do this? It's because they—you—too are lost in their own way. They have lost that sense of stewardship and sharing that God wants and the church teaches. They, too, are off the track, separated from the kind of life—the life of concern and being-for-others—that is what it really means to be one of God's flock and part of the church. A minister is charged to recall his own people from their lostness as much as he is to seek out the lost outside the church. There is to be rejoicing when the church members refind themselves and are returned truly to God's own flock.

To be a good shepherd to his own people, a minister not only has to remind them of the path and pasture where they should be. He needs to go where they are and seek them out and help them get unsnagged from the thickets that trap them. Someone outside a maze can see better than the people in it how to escape; that's why we can't save ourselves and need God.

I don't mean to play God, but maybe I can help you better understand and recognize your lostness and better find the path back to where you belong. People may not feel lost, but a minister can help them to this recognition, a necessary first step toward moving beyond their present plight. I can help you diagnose (so you can move beyond) those snares in your life that hold you back, those fears to be open to other people and to other lifestyles, those clingings to fixed and settled ways of life, to a standard of living and a lifestyle that hold the people in close bondage. I can help you measure those things that measure your lostness, to discover just how far you are from the open pastures and pathways of God. Just as, in order to minister to the lost out there in the world, we first must recognize their need, so also for the lost among us in the church: We first must recognize just how lost *we* are.

But there are paths out of this lostness, too. God's grace provides these paths, and it is a minister's joy to help express that grace and to lead people to and along these paths. There is just as much rejoicing in heaven when one of the church people is brought home as for anyone else. Heaven awaits that rejoicing. I yearn to feel that joy.

The minister then went on to talk about the specific project, the day-care center for children of working mothers, which he identified as the path God was providing them now to find their way back into his ways.

One Year Later: The Second Lost Sheep Sermon

What does it feel like to be lost? You do feel off the path and away from open places, just as the story suggests. You feel in tight closed places, caught, not able to move the way you want. You have some sense that there is a kind of life, a place in life, that is meant just for you, where you will feel well and at home. But you are not there. Perhaps that place is in memory and you feel you have left it—or perhaps been pushed out—or perhaps that place is still in hope and is a "not yet" rather than a "once upon a time." It is a place of promises, a promised place. It is a place that has been promised to you and a place you have promised to occupy. It is not exactly that these promises are broken. But despite the promises, you are not there.

I have discovered these feelings in my own attempts to be a minister. I know how I should function, but I don't always fulfill my expectations. I end many days feeling I am not much of a minister, at least not yet. That is especially true in my experience in the day-care project, which many of you have lived through with me. The vision of the project—the church at its best in reaching out to meet social and personal needs —seemed and still seems so clear and simple. Yet it is not happening that way; it is arousing more needs than it meets—

and a church project, too! Everyone involved feels the same kind of frustration of feeling caught and unable to make it feel different, and knowing they should.

Second, feeling lost involves some strange mixture of feeling both victimized and guilty. It happened *to* me. I did not lose myself. I, in fact, was on the path, maybe still am, but obstacles have loomed in front of me. I feel beset, stranded, maybe even betrayed and abandoned. It feels as though others have let me down, and in plain fact they have. Some of us have talked this through thoroughly in the day-care project, where we have recognized that it isn't anyone's fault, because everybody feels caught and displaced and off balance and not doing and being as they wish, and letting each other down. Yet along with the grief, and sometimes even the beginnings of anger, in this loneliness of feeling stranded, of feeling pushed off the path, there still is unaccountably the strange overwhelming sense of personal guilt. Even though I really know it has happened *to* me, I still feel terribly guilty, as though it was all my fault. That guilt has to be taken seriously; yet, as we all know, it is so hard to sort out what I really need to feel guilty about from the extra load of guilt I too easily take on myself.

Third, feeling lost makes me feel scared and panicked. Off balance and off the path, I feel vulnerable and fragile. The main way I express this is in being defensive, in trying to claim a power and a strength and puff myself up by pushing other people around. I throw around blame and orders. It is easy to try to make myself feel and look stronger and on the right path by treating everybody else as even weaker and more lost. One way to get over feeling like a lost sheep is to act as though you are the shepherd; I happen to know a minister who did this in a sermon on this text a year ago. If you try to act like the shepherd, you can pretend you are really back on the path and in charge.

One of the symptoms of not feeling in charge of yourself is to try to get in charge of others.

But fourth, the most important part of really feeling lost is that you come not really to *feel* lost. Even when we feel lost, God doesn't think of us as lost, and by living into our lost-ness, we can come to think of ourselves as God thinks of us. The parable speaks of the shepherd rejoicing. God's rejoicing is not the rejoicing of relief. For God, our lostness is not a cliff-hanger that leaves God in anxious suspense. Even when we feel lost, God perceives us as part of the flock and rejoices in that. God is not like the anxious parent or the anxious spouse who is afraid that the child one is raising may not make it and who communicates this mistrust and anxiety with all manner of helpfulness and "good shepherding." Such good shepherding communicates exactly the mistrust that motivates it; it communicates the perception of the other as weak and needy and lost. Such perception makes us feel all the more needy and lost; thus the sinister demeaning effect of so much good shepherding. God's care is not like that at all. God sees us as consistently part of the flock and communicates this caring in a way that makes us feel enabled and strengthened and empowered and found. With God we are found out not dragged out. God's rejoicing reaches to us where we are; he is not conditionally waiting for us to be brought where he is. Studies in schoolrooms have shown that when teachers are informed that their students have high in-telligence, the teachers treat the students in such a way that actually increases their intelligence. That's how God treats us, as being already his people, thus enabling us to become so. God doesn't close in on us in our lostness in a way that makes us aware of our problems and our weakness so much as he stands by, gives us room, and makes us feel his power within ourselves.

Two Approaches to Ministry

The two sermons differ drastically in:

· The *posture* the minister takes toward the people (and asks
  them to take toward others).
· Where *power* is located.
· Who is expected to make *promises* to whom.
· How the people are *perceived* and are asked to perceive
  themselves.
· The place that the *project* (a day-care center) takes in the
  aims of the minister and the life of the congregation and
  in the relation between minister and congregation.

Posture. In the first sermon the minister is separate from the
people and over them. (And as he asks them to imitate him,
he asks them to be separate from and over those to whom they
are to minister.) He knows more about them than they know
about themselves, about what is wrong with them, and about
how to remedy it. But what he knows he knows from observing
them not from examining himself, because his posture is as the
expert, as the guide, as the shepherd. He poses as immune to
the ills that beset them. Any separation the people may feel
from the project he proposes is a separation from the minister
who so closely identifies with the project and hence a separation from their best selves, of which the minister is custodian
and exemplar.

In the second sermon the minister is *with* the people (and
as he asks them to imitate him, he asks them to be with those
to whom they would minister). He listens to them, but he
speaks much about himself. He knows himself and his plight;
and he supposes that, since they share far more of the same
plight than not, by speaking of himself he enables them more

to understand themselves. Any separation they may feel from the project is not a separation from the minister, for he no longer identifies with the project but shares the ambivalences. Their posture is one of standing together observing the strain and ambivalences and wondering together what they mean and what new moves they suggest. If anyone is lost, they are lost together; if anyone finds the way out, they do it together.

In the first sermon the minister's finger is pointed at the people. In the second it is touching his own chin or scratching his own head, musing. In the first sermon the minister crowds the people; he herds them, as a good shepherd should. In the second sermon he leaves them room. In the first sermon the people have trouble seeing the path, because the minister is standing so squarely in it and calling attention to himself. In the second sermon the minister steps aside, and leaves them room to discern the path. In the first sermon the separation between minister and people is a hierarchical one; the minister stands farther ahead on the path and summons the people to bridge the distance between them. In the second sermon the separation between minister and people is lateral; he steps aside not as abandonment but as a gesture of encouragement and confidence, to give them room. They are to move ahead not toward *him*.

Power. In the first sermon the minister's superior posture implies his superior power. His is the special wisdom and skill and insight and calling. Without him the people are more helpless than with him, and they need to depend on him. Any resistance that people may show toward the project (and hence to the minister) is a measure of their weakness or wrongness. With the minister's help, and especially by aligning themselves with his project, they can remedy this weakness and wrongness.

In the second sermon the minister has no special power, except what becomes available to him as one of the people.

Nor does the project. They all have power—and responsibility —to perceive and to pursue the proper paths. Any resistance by them to the project is a signal of a power at work in them that needs to be respected and heeded, marshalled and employed. The minister signals his respect for the messages and directions in their ambivalences by searching for the meaning and guidance in his own. The power in their resistance to the project holds at least as much promise of finding a saving pathway as does the project itself.

Promises. In the first sermon the people must make the promises, and keep them, as a condition for their well-being. It is a classical ploy of parents and others who hold power insecurely to give a double message: You must promise to do what I am confidently assuring you you are incapable of doing. This is the message the minister, like many, many before him, is giving. It is a message Paul found in the Law. It is a demeaning and disempowering message. Heads I win; tails you lose. You must; you can't. It is a message to which the Protestant mistrust of mediators and machinery and vehicles of salvation leaves us especially prone. With grace so elusive salvation is on a do-it-yourself basis, and do-it-yourself is the flimsiest of bases. Resistance to the project, declining to promise or failing to keep promises to it, becomes a serious flaw, a measure of lostness, of being off the path of grace.

In the second sermon the promises are made by God, and they are unconditional. The promises hold, regardless of what promises people make or break in response. The refusal or breaking of a promise to a particular project does not change God's promise but can be perceived as appropriate experimentation in ways to apprehend and comprehend that promise. Because it is *God's* promises that prevail, no other promises claim such absolute sovereignty, neither the promise the minister sees in or makes to the project—nor the promises he asks the people to make to it. Such "permissiveness" always seems troubling when the people are perceived as weak or wrong without the power of the minister or surrogate, or without keeping promises for him. But such permissiveness is ennobling and enabling whenever it is perceived as a signal of the power offered to the people as part of God's promise. The people are perceived as already among the found, as already belonging to the flock, as already on the path.

Perception. In the first sermon people who do not feel lost are perceived and treated as lost and helpless and weak and wrong. If you don't feel lost, you should. In the second sermon people are allowed to feel lost if they do and in whatever way they do, but they are not treated that way by the minister because they are not perceived that way by the minister or by God. If you do feel lost, you needn't. It is not so much a matter of what is said as how it is said. In the first sermon the manner of the minister is essentially that of the self-righteous adult scolding the bad child. The minister assumes a role such that the only way to relate to him is to assume the reciprocal role and accept being a bad child. In the second sermon things are quite different. The minister assumes a role such that the way to relate to him is to fill the space he leaves with the role of a responsible adult, maturely searching out one's destiny. In the first sermon the vacuum or chaos is filled by the paths specifically supplied by the minister. That is the evidence of grace. In the second sermon the vacuum or chaos is embraced as somehow of lesser significance than the fact that restoration is already assured by a power that has conquered far more chaos than anyone present knows. *That* is the measure of grace.

Project. In the first sermon the minister identifies his own vocation and his people's specifically in terms of a particular project. They are called to endorse and agree and join and labor according to the minister's blueprints, for their own good—and for his, the world's, and God's. Energies are focused—constricted, actually—in a two-dimensional world: There is no room for movement except to be for or against the project. Being for or against the project—in one's votes or behavior or conversation or private thoughts—is the best approximation one can project onto this two-dimensional space of one's actual energies. Were energies not so constricted in this two-dimensional space defined by the project, then some energies would likely be going in other directions.

In the second sermon the project exists just as significantly, but it does not define the space. It exists in a space defined by the people's own searching and working out of their callings. In the mood established by the first sermon people's reactions, such as attendance at a committee meeting, are measured with reference to the project. In the mood set by the second sermon the project becomes measured by people's reactions. The project is one occasion, one among many possibilities, in which people discover both discouraging and encouraging things about themselves and from which they grow. The project is an occasion for growth not the criterion by which it is measured.

As a result of the first sermon people of Grace Church enlisted in the project and also had some strong, though unconscious, fears or furies mobilized by it, eventually to be played out in relation to it. After the second sermon the project lost its place as the focus for anxious strivings of various kinds. It seemed to carry itself not as the guarantee of salvation for anyone but just as a day-care center. People found themselves sharing less disguisedly their anxiousness and strivings and addressing the meaning in these moods, even—maybe especially—the moods of no-saying.

The Story of the Day-Care Center

The project of ministry to which Tom Goddard's first sermon summoned Grace Church was a good project, addressed to a real need. The rest of this chapter tells of the life and death of that project, and of the rebirth and transformation of that project into still deeper ministry.

As minister, as a good shepherd, Tom Goddard initiated the project and was skillful and effective in leading the people to share his vision and to develop the project. The congregation did adopt it, made it theirs, and made commitments to it. Then after a time of yes-saying and partnership between minister and people, the people began to say no. Sometimes subtly and even unconsciously, sometimes overtly and even defiantly, most often with apathy, the people began to renege on their commitments and to let the project flounder and fail. So far, a typical episode in the life of a church. The minister felt stranded and angry, "lost," perhaps, but unconsciously so. Privately he fumed at the people's no. Publicly he tried to recall them to their earlier yes, to remind them of the vision and of the worth of the project and of their commitment to it. He tried to return the lost sheep to the flock and the path.

But the story is included for what happened next, for the ministry that began *after* the people said no and the minister was stunned, *after* the people became "lost" and Tom God- dard a stranded shepherd—the ministry celebrated in the sec- ond sermon. The story is not here for whatever ministry was frustrated by the people's no but for the ministry that was built upon that no. The story is not here to recount the minister's efforts to attack the no, to undo it and return it to yes; that, too, is too common to recount. The story is here—ministry was present—because the minister took the no seriously, ac- cepted it as no, listened to the message in the no, joined the people in feeling lost, listened with them to the message in the gospel addressed to all of them: God's yes spoken to their common no.

Lest the reader expect, either wanting or fearing, an account of ministry that is dramatically novel, breathtakingly fresh and adventurous, let the warning (or the reassurance) here be offered that the ministry described may seem dramatically ordinary. The ministry that was built upon taking seriously the no was a ministry of word—especially Gospel—and of sacrament and of caring and of gathering and of outreach that may seem quite conventional in the telling, as conventional as the second "Lost Sheep" sermon. Certainly it was more conventional than the day-care project whose floundering precipitated this ministry. But also it was no less radical, for it was a ministry of word and of caring and of gathering that had a focus and a sharing and an intensity and a sense of reality and an effect greater than if minister and people had not lived together and hurt together and ministered together through the project and through the no-saying. The ministry discovered in the debris of the day-care project was more radical than that project, too, in the ways it did find to reach out to those to whom the project was directed.

Any radicalness of ministry suggested by this chapter and by this book is not in inventing new responses to human predicaments; it does take seriously the conviction that the Gospel can and must heal human brokenness. Any radicalness is not in finding new needs and plights for the Gospel to address; people persist in their alienation from the best in themselves, from each other, and from God. Any radicalness is in the simple supposition that such brokenness, such alienation, such need for the Gospel is found in the very midst of the people of God, at the very heart of the workings of minister and people with each other and with their struggle to find faith and vocation as a people. Any radicalness is in believing that such disruption and alienation—precisely at the point at which the people are banding together to overcome disruption and alienation—is to be expected and is even to be greeted. It is not obstacle to ministry but occasion for ministry, deepened ministry, focused ministry, more intensely shared and committed ministry. Any radicalness here is in the conviction that the lost *are* found—even when the lost are strayed would-be good shepherds.

Yes-Saying: First Commitments

Tom Goddard vividly remembers when he first got the idea for the day-care center. It was one of those rare "ah-ha!" experiences, when suddenly everything seemed to come together in his mind, and he knew he had a good idea. Tom was glancing through his denomination's monthly publication when his eye caught the short report of a day-care center organized in the parish house of a downtown church. Although Grace was a suburban church, in a very different community, Tom could immediately see exactly how and why Grace should undertake this. He saw the project unfolding spontaneously before him, meeting many needs in the church and in the community and giving his own ministry a needed shot in the arm. He knew that the people and the church would enthusiastically adopt it as a good idea, and he was right; they did. It met the needs he and they had to be good shepherds.

There are many reasons that made Tom—and very soon, many of his church members—give such a quick yes to this project. It is important to look at some of these reasons here in order to recognize the degree of commitment the project first evoked from the congregation and also to recognize the depth of anguish and frustration when the people began to say no. A project with this many reasons for it, and so much initial enthusiasm for it, simply ought not to develop the no-saying it did.

Tom had a long-standing commitment to a ministry of service to the community—to be a good shepherd—and so did Grace Church; there had been much talk about this when the pulpit committee first sought him out, and there had been much rhetoric in his installation service about a minister and people together finding avenues of faithful service in their community. But these commitments had found little expression while Tom had been at Grace Church, and the church's ministry was largely self-contained and self-directed. Most projects of outreach into the community seemed too grand and too fearful.

But the day-care center seemed just right. It was a modest and feasible way to be good shepherds. The day-care center project readily bypassed many of the suspicions and fears on which previous ventures in mission had floundered. Children are intuitively appealing, their need for care is personal and individual, and they would be coming into the parish house to be served. (The church people were always a bit threatened when they were asked to go out and confront larger social institutions, and when they were asked to find some way to serve more remote groups, in the ghetto, for instance, with whom they had little personal contact.) The project asked people to give services and time, with which they were more generous than money. Though it was going to reach people outside the church—there were few working mothers in the church—they were people living in their same suburb who seemed not greatly different in lifestyle and values; after all, the mothers were working. It was going to use resources of the church and activities already familiar; the day-care center would be much like the Sunday school. In short, the project was a meaningful venture at community service, but one modest enough to minimize apprehension and to maximize enthusiasm in the congregation.

So Tom Goddard was enthusiastic about this project, and justifiably so. This was something the church should and could and would do. Tom could immediately and easily picture the scene in the parish house—the children happy and well cared for and well loved by the many willing volunteers in the space recently redesigned and redecorated by other volunteers from the church. He could picture himself and the congregation, emboldened and reassured by this one venture, rediscovering that they *could* exercise an outreach ministry to the community, moving on to other, bolder projects. He could picture the church becoming known, both by its members and by outsiders, as the church with an effective social conscience; this is how he had long envisioned his ministry. He could picture the attention the day-care center would get in the local newspapers, in the denominational monthly, and maybe in his seminary publication. He could even picture himself happily confronting the vigorous champion of women's rights who regularly made him feel guilty for not doing more himself. Now he would feel her approval.

"How delighted he is then! He lifts it on to his shoulders and home he goes to call his friends and neighbors together. . . ."

In his enthusiasm, in these hopes and daydreams, and in the care and energy with which he went about introducing the program to the church, Tom obviously had an investment in it. By no means all of his personal or vocational eggs were in this one basket; but he was trusting some substantial part of himself to the project. He would feel more faithful in ministry, more fulfilled in vocation, a bit more easy in conscience—more ready to hold his head up as the minister he wanted to be before his congregation, his colleagues, his seminary professors, and his God—if this project succeeded.

Tom Goddard not only invested his enthusiasm and his daydreams and his hopes and his intentions for effective ministry. He also invested his skill. He was a skillful and careful minister, a *good* shepherd. He had identified a project that he knew would be attractive and acceptable to most people in his congregation. He carefully identified the individuals and the groups with whom it would be important to share his thinking. He patiently spent time with these people, introducing his ideas to them, hearing them out. He anticipated the questions each would have and had thought out his own responses. He was open and ready to let them modify and refine his ideas. He thought ahead to know exactly what further assignments and responsibilities he wanted to ask each person to undertake. He anticipated just how much and just how little direction each person would want and need, and he had some practical advice —whom to see, what to say—for those who were going to need and heed it. Soon Tom Goddard and his people were in genuine and vigorous partnership on this project. If asked, the people would have remembered it was Tom's idea in the first place, but they would have insisted that it was now *their* project, part of the ministry of Grace Church, not just part of Tom's ministry. Tom was a skillful and careful minister.

Tom's skill, like the modesty and attractiveness of the proposal itself, is important to emphasize here, not just so we can understand and believe the ready and enthusiastic yes with which the congregation first responded. Remembering Tom's gentle skill will also help us better savor the misery and mystery of the no when it begins to appear. When I begin to describe the no—the resistance and the apathy and the objections and the sabotage—that began to cluster around this project and to smother it, you may react at first with a feeling of easy recognition: "That is the kind of opposition social activists always get in churches." But Tom Goddard was not a stereotypical social activist. He did not deserve the rebuff that is deserved by the naive, roughshod social activist who, with the facade of prophet, angrily and arbitrarily inflicts on people judgments and demands they are unprepared to comprehend. Tom received the rebuff without deserving it; thus the depth of the anguish and frustration and cause for anger and resentment Tom experienced.

However, that he received the rebuff without deserving it is precisely what opened the way for ministry and guided it. That the rebuff could not plausibly be attributed to anything he had done freed him from defensiveness and guilt. More important, that the rebuff could not plausibly be attributed to anything he had done is precisely what prompted his query as to where the rebuff did come from. It came from within the people and carried messages about them, messages about matters in their inner lives that invited and required ministry, messages about their inner lives that guided that ministry. The inappropriateness, the unfairness of the no, then, is exactly what induces misery and exactly what induces ministry.

(But we should note in passing that, even if Tom *had* deserved the rebuff, there still would have been need and room for ministry. The no can be a response both to high-handed tactics that block ministry and deserve the no and also to inner torments that people are bringing to the episode and that invite ministry. Even if the high-handed tactics and not the day-care center idea itself were the trigger, the gun is still loaded in advance. The people, apparently, are already charged with an explosiveness. That explosiveness, which happens to disrupt life in the church, also is there ready and able to disrupt life in many other places. So it is what requires and invites and guides ministry.)

But before the people began to say no—and thereby to frustrate the minister and to invite and guide ministry—they said yes, a resounding yes. They, too, wanted to be good shepherds and welcomed this way to be so. The official board approved the project not routinely but with enthusiasm and with their own ideas. The fourth and fifth grade Sunday school classes readily agreed "to share our rooms with other kids," cleared off their bulletin board, put up a welcome sign, and made plans to come visit "the other kids." A modest low-key campaign yielded pledges of enough money to support the project. Members of the house committee spent two weekends building some supply closets and repainting one of the rooms and made plans for designing and building some climbing bars outside when the weather got better. A "grandmother's club" readily organized and became the core staff of volunteers for care and for transportation. A director was hired, and one trustee readily took care of the necessary approval by the health authorities and the fire marshal. The teams that called in homes to invite children came back speaking happily about the chance "to meet new people." Members of the congregation were proud of the attention in the local newspaper, and people frequently were heard bragging proudly to their friends about the project.

The yes *was* resounding. Minister and people seemed to be in full and enthusiastic partnership. The minister had taken the first step, but the people soon were in stride with him. The minister had taken a modest leap from his trapeze, but he had been caught and received not stranded and left to drop; he and people were swinging together. So it went for several weeks.

No-Saying: Resistance Emerges

Then the signs of resistance appeared, so familiar to any minister as perhaps not to be noticed at first. Resistance seems the normal way of life in the church, and perhaps it is; from the point of view of this book it is precisely what is normal and expected and to be attended to as the occasion for ministerial response. The first no message that Tom recalls came quite indirectly: The fourth grade Sunday school teacher said that one of the girls in her class said that her mother said that she shouldn't have to take down her picture from the bulletin board. An irrational and trivial nuisance in the life of the church and in the way of this project, indeed, but the teacher happened to pay enough attention to it to mention it to Tom. Tom had managed to convey to the teacher the impression that such things were important and could be constructively responded to. And Tom happened to pay enough attention to the teacher's report to call on the mother to see what was up.

This was a family on the edges of the church and one that had not been involved in the day-care center planning in any way. What Tom learned from that mother gave him clues that helped him understand, as he might never have done otherwise, many of the other signals of resistance that were shortly to appear. The mother unleashed a barrage of indignation: Her daughter ought not to have to give up things for "those others"; her daughter ought not to have to go visit "those others." As Tom listened, for over an hour, he realized that he had never before quite sensed the precariousness with which some people clung to their own station in life, a precariousness easily threatened by the presence, especially by the moving presence, of those a notch or two below on the social ladder. For this woman the sharing of the bulletin board—to her an imposed and enforced sharing—triggered fears of encroachment that beset her frequently. It triggered her annoyance that at the local supermarket people who dressed differently and spoke differently and seemed to buy different foods and to have more children now crowded her at the delicatessen counter and in the aisles; "they" were crowding her out of "her" store. The bulletin board triggered her fears aroused by the arrival of a black family in her neighborhood, the superstitions and prejudices that saw this as a threat to those values on which she relied mostly for her well-being, namely, property values and the value system and lifestyle she wanted to pass on, essentially unexamined, from her own parents to her children. Her life was precariously bastioned; mixing and yielding to lives that were noticeably different was very threatening. She felt a lost sheep with a vengeance and so tried hard, in her own way, to herd. (If Tom recognized himself in this posture, it wasn't conscious—yet.)

Her needs for focus and for affirmation, for the assurance

and direction of the Gospel, were too overwhelming to be addressed decisively in one call. But by neglecting to defend the plans for the bulletin board and for visiting, and by hearing and opening and accepting her needs, Tom did a lot.

He also learned a lot. He preached the next Sunday far more eloquently and compassionately and meaningfully than he would have otherwise on the theme of "Seek ye first the kingdom of Heaven. . . ." He made it a warm invitation and not another command. Many people heard this message well, even though the woman was not there to hear it. Also, Tom rediscovered the importance of talking about such matters individually, because such things as a day-care center mean different things to different people—a conscience-easing chance to make good on service commitments for one person, a chance to spend mornings constructively and less alone for another, but for this woman a reminder of serious and frightening social threats. Being moved in on and supplanted by "others" was not the only threat Tom was to hear about in the coming months. But having heard her out at length, he was far more attuned to the frights and the needs within this and forthcoming signs of resistance.

Other no was indeed forthcoming, most of it subtle, much of it seeming to be standard, pure no, pure resistance, without any obvious message. Tom listened anyway. Planning meetings were less well attended, but "this is a busy time." Some pledges were unpaid, and the workers did not come back to finish their painting or to build the jungle gym. But such looseness to commitments may seem such a standard way of life in a church as not to attract notice or invite inquiry. Tom wondered what the people might be communicating by this decommitment, but there was no easy opportunity to inquire or to respond. Perhaps thanks to the fourth-grader's mother, Tom was more ready to suppose that there *was* something important behind this resistance and within it and less ready simply to respond with his own grief for being stranded. To a friend he found himself musing not just about what the apathy meant to him, a letdown after a setup, but also about what it meant to the people. When he said to his friend *"Why do they back down?"* he meant the why? at least as much as genuine inquiry as he meant it as protest; his why? was an honest why? and not just an angry one.

But some of the forms of resistance were more revealing. Some of the members of the "grandmother's club" were willing to be open with each other, with Tom, and with some of the working mothers. "Sometimes their hair isn't even combed in the morning," they would say to each other. To Tom it would be "I just don't get as much fun out of this as I thought I would. It's hard to get acquainted with some of the kids. I guess I am getting old. I used to get along well with children." And to the mothers they were more controlled but clear: "You are thirty minutes late picking up Elizabeth. But that's perfectly all right. I'm sure you had a good reason." The differences in lifestyles were more disconcerting than anyone had supposed. Some of the grandmothers began to drop out of their work.

Tom felt a personal disappointment. He had especially delighted in the warm enthusiasm these older women had offered to the project. He had spent considerable effort and tact in recruiting them, and their response was rewarding to him and reassuring that the project was a good one and would work well. The initial warmth of their concern for the children had made him feel that this would be a day-care center with a difference because it was in a Christian church—good shepherds for Jesus. He envisioned emphasizing this point when he wrote the report he planned for the denominational monthly magazine. So Tom did feel a special disappointment when the women's enthusiasm cooled.

"Not You!": The Standard Response

At first, he tried to counter this disappointment and this cooling by urging them and by recalling them to their earlier commitment and warmth. "Be good shepherds." His first reaction was to minimize their de-commitment and to minimize the discomfort and distance with which they expressed it: "Oh, you are not so old. You've seen uncombed hair before. These mothers *are* busy; that's why we are here to help. I think you really enjoyed playing that extra half hour with Elizabeth." Taking their attention away from their discomfort, he tried to return it to their commitment: "Remember how important this is and how we promised each other to stick with it." He preached a sermon about being suffering servants. He cajoled and argued and pleaded as skillfully and energetically as he had first time around: Don't say no; say yes, again.

His response was the standard response of clergy—so long as they are acting like parents and other good shepherds—of pointing the finger and saying, "Not you! That's not like you. You can't be that way. I will not have you that way. I will call you back to the real you." There was also an element of "Not you, too!" Another traitor or defector whom I did not expect. *Et tu Brute.* You are friend turned antagonist. So I must treat you as the wayward adversary so that I can bring you back to the true ways, my ways.

Tom first practiced the ministry of "Not you" standing strongly as the good shepherd of the day-care center: He was the staunch custodian of that project and of the consciences and commitments that should be directed to it. The strayed would be returned. That was his job; he was the minister.

But Tom was not exclusively program oriented. He was also a pastor to these people. He could sense personal distress lurking in their waywardness. So he shifted from the good shepherd of the program to the good shepherd of the women. He began to talk with them privately about the personal problems he thought might be hinted at in their difficulties with the working mothers and the day-care center. He asked one woman if her husband was back to drinking too much again. He was sympathetic toward another about her arthritis. He hinted strongly to another his suspicion that she might be worried and guilty about her pending decision to transfer her mother to a nursing home. To still another, he talked about her recent absences from church. Though personal and pastoral, not program oriented, these were all still responses of "Not you." They were still responses of the good shepherd designating the others as lost so that he could herd them and heal them. He was just changing the grounds on which he intended to move them from no-saying to yes-saying.

This shift from program diagnosis and remedy to pastoral diagnosis and remedy is not what this book recommends, although it could well be mistaken for that. It still is not taking the no seriously as having its own legitimate meaning and guidance, even call to ministry. It is, instead, to hear the resistance as an indirect cry for help. Perhaps that is what it sometimes is, and it may be good pastoral strategy to be alert to such pleas. But it also may be an arrogant assumption—that a woman's discomfort in a parish program or resistance to it somehow represents "trouble" or "problems" in her life that the minister needs to move in on and to solve. This is a common maneuver that men make against women, men ministers against women parishioners, to discount any objection or resistance as a symptom, betraying a disease the man/minister will heal. To try to track a no spoken in church back into personal problems is to miss the call that is in the no fully as much as smoothing it over does. Women call this maneuver a power trip by the man, and they are right. Tom could not respect and attend to the no-saying and listen to the calls to ministry in it because he was still so determined to be a strong minister. He was saying, "You are not yourself when you complain about uncombed hair and all the rest. I will help you be yourself by helping you solve your problems."

The women *were* being themselves in their complaints and their resistance, more fully themselves than in any simple yes-saying of punctuality and steady smiles. And they were being themselves, responding to real events, in the day-care center. To hear the meaning and the call to ministry in their complaints, Tom had to take these complaints seriously, and to take them seriously in the terms in which they expressed themselves: uncombed hair and tardy pickups and all the rest. Tom could not suppose that the meaning was only in undoing the no and making it yes, or that the meaning was off somewhere in personal and family life.

Tom's first response was to suppress the no—and to urge the women to do likewise—to recall and cling to the yes—and to urge the women to do likewise—saying "Not you" to the no; and his second response was to divert the no into a problem to be solved, again saying "Not you" to the no. But he did come to a new response, which was to accept their gentle no as valid, meaningful, important, and to explore it for clues to ministry—and to enable the women to do likewise.

This new response came in a turning point sudden and dramatic enough to be called truly a conversion. Like all conversions, there was a startling moment of confession, a radical letting go of some old, firmly entrenched ways of understanding and conducting oneself—a confession of their wrongness —and a sudden opening up to new ways—a confession of faith and trust in their rightness. If his standard ministerial response was the message of "Not you," the would-be good shepherd, he was able to discover a new and powerful ministry, the ministry of "Me, too," the ministry of becoming a fellow lost sheep. But before this could happen, there happened the dramatic moment of confession and conversion, which Tom experienced as "Not me!" He really did feel lost, and said so. It was not just a new posture.

"Not Me!": Confession and Conversion

It all started with some toy animals left strewn on the floor. Tom overheard a couple of his "grandmothers" gently grumbling about the scatter left behind at the end of the day by the children and their mothers. Tom lost his cool. He strode into the midst of the grandmothers and, wordlessly and vigorously —one might have said even violently—began scooping up toys. When he had an armload, he unloaded them in the toy box, then turned and unloaded on the grandmothers: "It's not all that hard to pick up a few toys. We have to be willing to go a second mile. That's what this project is all about. The kids are not used to having toys like this to deal with, and the mothers are still shy around here. They are still our guests, and feel it, and we have to be willing to be the gracious hosts. If we don't have a little grace to share, what's it all for? But you do. I know you do." Tom embellished this tirade liberally with biblical quotations: "Do unto others. . . ." "Except as ye become as little children. . . ." "What does the Lord require of you but. . . ." And a great many more. He peppered the tirade with especially pointed "Not you!" remarks: "If we can't count on you. . . ." "We talked about troubles like this when we started and you said you could handle them. . . ." "It's hard to keep everything else running when the main gear breaks down. . . ." (And he thought but didn't say, "How can I be a minister if you won't be the church?")

The women were stunned, and so was Tom. The outburst spent, they all stooped and picked up toys, wordlessly and sullenly. Tom found himself on his knees, and some surprising reflections came to him in his stunned state. "What am I doing? That doesn't sound like me. That's not me." He startled himself and the women even more by sharing this "Not me" confession with them. When the toys were all picked up, he stayed on his knees. He didn't apologize, exactly. He just opened himself. As must be a true and necessary condition for all confessions and conversions, he felt himself safely surrounded by love. His voice was low. "That didn't sound like Tom Goddard. That sounded like a raving maniac. Maybe I am a raving maniac. But I feel more like that scared looking little bunny rabbit you just put in the box."

So, having confessed the "Not me," he began to explore it and to discover the "Me, too."

"I guess your own irritations and frustrations, which you were able to express, touched some of my own, which have been dammed up until the dam just burst. I guess I have a whale of a lot invested in this project going well, and I am not so sure—even less sure than you are—that it is going well. If I put you down that hard, I must really have been needing to put myself up, pull myself up. I must have felt way down. I guess I was trying to scold myself, too, to make myself feel better about all the picking up I seem to have to do, going the second mile, filling in the gaps, and smiling about it all the time. . . . Wow, I can't believe I just said that. But it feels right, and good. I guess I really have bottled up a lot, and you got it all." Then, for the first time, he looked up with a warm, almost twinkling look, and found some warm looks coming back. One woman came over and put a hand on his shoulder, and others seemed to be doing the same with their eyes. No one spoke for a while. No one seemed to feel the need to talk about Tom and his outburst. What he had said spoke for itself.

When one woman did speak, it seemed irrelevant. It was irrelevant to the content of what Tom had been saying, but not to its mood. Openness breeds openness, confession breeds confession, grace breeds grace. "Me, too" ministry does not mean that people imitate each other, only that they each share. Deep responding to deep, plight to plight, one woman began speaking, slowly and softly, as in meditation. "How can they be so happy all of the time? My sister was always like that, and I always wanted to be. But I would only get sober and tell her to sober up too. My husband, too; I keep telling him, 'Oh Charles.' I guess that's what I do with the kids, too, telling them to sober up when I really mean to be telling myself to cheer up. . . ."

Her remarks were surrounded by silence, too. No one felt the need to "shepherd," to answer plights, to reassure despair. The despair was acceptable and even seemed to breed its own strength. If these were lost sheep huddling together—and they were—the discovery was that even lost sheep have resources to untangle themselves and find their way. The ministry of "Not me" and "Me, too" had an unlocking and refreshing power. Tom and the women felt the power of the Spirit more present in their midst at this moment of open receptiveness than ever in moments of Tom's efforts to conscript the Spirit.

So Tom found himself and found new reaches and depths of ministry in a spontaneous moment of lostness. In this moment of conversion Tom lost the need to prove himself good shepherd, to stand over and ahead of others. Seldom again did he respond to de-commitment, subtle or overt, with his previous standard response: calling and recalling people to the commitments he defined for them. Instead, he found the grace to move, even haltingly and unsurely, *with* the others, to feel a mutuality of need and of search and of grace. By being more open to his own distress and de-commitment—the no mixed with the yes in himself—he could be more open to others' distress and de-commitment and learn to hear the yes mixed with their no. By discovering that he could live with and through his own distress, he could minister with and through theirs. He could find a partnership, a covenant of ministry in shared search, even shared lostness. Ministry need not presuppose the unbalanced shepherd-sheep partnership in which the minister must be strong and the people weak but becoming strong under the minister's coaching. Ministry happens, too—maybe especially—when the minister displays weakness and either lets the people be weak, too, or credits their strength. The minister need not be a yes-sayer and a maker of yes-sayers, rejecting and denying the no-saying so abundant in both minister and people. The minister may be a fellow no-sayer, unlocking the power of the no, their shared no. Tom Goddard discovered new patterns of ministry in himself when he discovered that he could face his own grief and irritation and his need to muffle that grief by insisting on saying and hearing yes, because he could thereby discover new powers in the people, in their grief and irritation.

Now let us look at some of the fruits of that moment of conversion, the effects of a style of ministry of joining lost sheep in their lostness to the point of discovering the meaning in their lostness and evoking the power in it.

The Ministry of "Me, Too": Lost and Finding

"It's hard to get acquainted with some of the kids. I guess I am getting old. . . ." When one of the grandmothers said this gentle no to Tom, he first heard it as a small piece of the machinery of his project slowing down and needing some oiling and energizing. So he was first tempted to smooth over and to pep up; that was his familiar way of dealing with roughness and downness. So he almost said, "You are just the kind of person these kids need and respond to. I have seen how well you get along with them. They really like you, though some may be shy about showing that." *Why* feel down and say no—the why of protest, not of inquiry, the why that means don't: *Don't* feel down; *don't* say no. Your feelings don't match my feelings or the way I want you to feel or what I think you have felt. They are disruptive feelings that I want to eliminate by classifying as wrong. Let's think positively. Let's think yes. Be good shepherds.

The most standard way of trying to make people feel up is to put down their feelings of being down. People may comply for the moment, but the long-range effect is the "double down."

What the "new" Tom Goddard did say sounded similar, but it had a very different intent and effect. He did ask why? But he meant it as a question and not as don't. In effect, "Are you lost sheep?" He did call attention to the discrepancy between the woman's down feeling and his own observation that she, in fact, seemed to be getting along well with the children. But noting the discrepancy was a way of accepting and emphasizing the down feelings not quashing them. It sounded like "Not you," and it almost was, except this time it really meant "Not all of you," as an invitation to hear more. Noting the discrepancy was a way of looking at the no squarely. The feelings of no and of down are valid and are all the more important and worth exploring because they don't match all the facts. Look for the message written in the roughness, don't try to smooth it over and erase the message. That's what Tom wanted to say when he said, "You do seem down today about the kids, even though it seems that you have been getting along with them pretty well."

"About the kids" was part of Tom's response because he resisted the temptation to be "pastoral," to divert the conversation to a "problem" that was exclusively hers, and not something they shared here and now. Tom was clear that the woman was feeling down *about the kids.*

The woman responded to the gentle inquiry. "Some days I guess they just seem rambunctious." Tom just listened. Whatever the rambunctiousness meant to her would come out.

"They get unruly and don't want to quiet down when we ask them, and they don't want to play the games we have planned for them."

"It makes you wonder what you are doing here," Tom reflected. "I sometimes wonder, too."

"Well, yes." She accepted the invitation to talk about herself, in this situation. There was some spark of anger, and perhaps she was a little anxious, that the children were different from her and from what she expected. These were the feelings that Tom had heard from the fourth-grader's mother. But beyond these feelings of anger and anxiety about *them* were stronger anxieties about herself. She wanted to tell Tom about the misgivings that she had that she was different from them and from what they expected. "Children used to be quiet for me, but then I used to be sure what they were like and what they wanted to do. These seem to get along fine without me. I want to call them to attention and back to our plans, but I am not sure that I should."

These misgivings blossomed into a wide range of distressing concerns, as Tom talked longer with her and with others. All of the feelings are common to the aging, but they came out especially strong as these women confronted the day-care kids. For one thing, there was a hint of the anger that Tom heard so strongly from the fourth-grader's mother that "they are taking over." In this case it was more the dilemma of the aging being crowded by new generations rather than one ethnic or economic group being crowded by another. But Tom noted that a profound fear was shared by these workers in the program, by himself, and by an opponent of it; all felt the risk of becoming abandoned sheep. Along with the anger, there were hints of the grief the women felt in losing authority and recognition and affection. They felt abandoned and stranded by the kids, just as Tom felt abandoned and stranded by the grandmothers. Here he and the grandmothers shared a grief, felt fellow lost sheep. More poignant than the anger or grief, there was a touch of envy and perhaps regret. In the rambunctiousness the women felt some "soul," which they had missed in their own lives, even in their childhood. Was there a possibility that these kids, and their mothers, who were taking over the space and time of the grandmothers were making better use of it than the grandmothers knew how to? In the disrupting no that she was hearing the woman was hearing the possibility of a new "call," which also was discomforting. In her ambivalence over whether to give the children tighter or looser rein, she was expressing uncertainty and frustration over the authority they would accord her; she was also expressing uncertainty and frustration over her contentment with her own life.

"We give them all this extra time by taking care of their children, and what do they do with it?" one grandmother once grumbled. "Sometimes I think these women have the right idea," another replied, admiring the greater independence and carefreeness of the working mothers. But for her to say that was to risk saying to herself that she may have lived out some of the wrong ideas. Perhaps the message she heard in the day-care center was not that life was partly passing her by now in her later years, but that life had partly passed her by *all* her years. For a woman to risk saying that, even to herself, she needs a church and a minister. In finding the bonds with others, the shared plights and open understanding that they found in these explorations of their no, these women found a church and a minister. How Tom Goddard further responded to this call for ministry will be seen later, after we look at some more conversations he had with members of the grandmothers' club.

When the grandmothers talked to themselves and not to Tom, they were more direct and open in their complaints, as in "sometimes their hair is not even combed in the morning." To the working mothers who were late picking up their children, they were clear about their grievance but also much more controlled and polite: "I'm sure that you had a good reason." When Tom began hearing complaints like this, he encouraged the women to say more about their grievances. He heard some more disapproval of the lifestyles of the working mothers: "I don't think they own any dresses." "Two don't even have husbands." He heard of many more incidents in which the grandmothers felt that the working mothers were not doing their part: They didn't stay long enough in the mornings to help the kids get used to being there; they forgot to bring the favorite toys they promised they would leave with their children; they interrupted the program during the day by phoning in to ask about their children.

Tom also heard a remarkable amount of self-righteousness: We always used to take care of our children properly; we get ourselves here on time in the morning; I have worked just as hard as these women have, without getting a salary, before there were machines to do all the housework. The unusual degree of pique and self-righteousness astounded Tom, as it grieved him. He was momentarily tempted to be the "good" shepherd, standing firm and calling the lost back to their proper roles of servanthood. But then he found it natural to abandon his "goodness" and firmness and to look for them where they were. The unusualness, the "wrongness" of the self-righteousness, which grieved him, also signaled to him that something important was lodged in this troubling outburst. He decided to look directly into it, to see if its message could be discerned: "This sounds more like the Girl Scouts' awards day for good deeds than like my grandmothers' club."

"Well, somebody has to appreciate us," one woman retorted, continuing to illustrate the self-righteousness more than exploring it. So Tom kept focusing on his melancholy surprise as a surprise and as a puzzle. "But you know how much you *are* appreciated. I hear the mothers say thank you every day. That can't be what all this patting on the back is about." If the feelings don't match the facts, or if the feelings don't match the explanation, then the feelings must be attended to as especially important, not reshaped to match the facts or the explanation. The shepherd goes where the lost are. Tom was genuinely lost in his puzzlement, without any ready answer or explanation, and didn't mind saying so. His puzzlement was a genuine invitation.

"Well, sure they say thank you, but you can't be sure they mean it. . . . (Tom waited.) It's often hard to know *what* they are thinking. It's hard to know where they're at."

"Or whether they are there at all." Tom ventured to expand their point and relate it to the complaints he heard about feeling abandoned.

One woman let these feelings carry her along. "Sometimes I wonder where other members of our committee are. Last Monday I hurried dishes and walked down to the church for a meeting, and no one was there when I got there."

So the conversation went on. The children and their mothers and others in the project had aroused a mixture of feelings in the women, feelings that were already present in them as women and as members of an older generation, feelings that interfered with their work in the day-care center, feelings that they began to signal in the various ways they were saying no to that work. They were feeling abandoned and stranded, bypassed and estranged, separated from their customary roles and stations, separated from those with whom they wanted to be in helping partnerships, separated from the centers of their own lives, separated from the centers that seemed to control the life about them, separated from possibilities in their own lives, possibilities that the working mothers and their children rekindled tantalizingly. The anguish was especially great because they felt they had been promised, and indeed deserved, place and partnership. The anguish was especially great because they felt they had lost access to remedy; they were not able to speak to or to be heard by the working mothers (and others), who were the estrangers and estranged. They felt loss and grief, but there was no one against whom they could effectively or properly feel aggrieved.

They felt twice separated from many others in their lives. First there was the separation from the children caused by the rowdiness of the children or by the tardiness of the committee members or the mothers. But then there was the more excruciating separation of having to swallow this affront or loss, of being unable to speak to others about it, of being helpless to find remedy. There was estrangement, and there was loneliness and the despair in the estrangement.

That's how Tom and the grandmothers discerned these encounters with themselves that were coded in their remarks about the uncombed hair and the tardy pickups and the rowdy children.

In hearing all this, the most important response Tom made was to say regularly to himself, "Me, too." As he heard and reflected the grandmothers' feelings, Tom found himself drawn powerfully out of the aloof observer-shepherd role and into these feelings, like suddenly recognizing his own face in the photograph of a crowd scene. "Me, too": He felt his own feelings of abandonment swallowed into the grandmothers' feelings of abandonment; and he no longer felt so alone. "Me, too": He felt his own frustrations and anger and yearning about promises hinted at and broken, opportunities missed (especially those about the day-care center), joined and completed by the grandmothers' wistful yearnings; and it was not nearly so hard to admit how lost he had actually felt. It was possible suddenly to feel an essential part of a genuine ongoing human enterprise—the searching of the lost, the wistful "might-have-beens" of the established—rather than feeling on the margins of things. He felt himself part of those who felt apart, that is, part of the majority. "Me, too": I am being crowded out of the space and role and crowded out of "my" day-care center—just as the grandmothers feel crowded out of "their" day-care center! Together, we feel squeezed out of those spots in which we feel comfortable and competent by others' inability to accept our comfort or to recognize our competence. And in the "Me, too" discovery Tom suddenly felt he again had a place, with the grandmothers. "Me, too": Those who seemed to be strong and against me are not. They are *like* me, feeling weak and in these feelings *with* me.

This transformation of mood released new energies for new ministry, a ministry of "Me, too": Energies he had spent in trying to reach the grandmothers, or to fend them off, or to establish himself—all of these energies could be released now that he saw that he and they were together, were established, in their lostness. The energies could be spent much more fruitfully and productively for the common good. It was all right to feel the way he did, because others did, too; it was not something to fret over and try to undo. This constant rediscovery of "Me, too" was a profound rediscovery over again of the freeing gospel, a reminder of the "conversion."

Whenever Tom would say "Me, too" to himself and experience the freedom of feeling plights recognized and shared, he would pass along this experience to the grandmothers. Now and then he would drop into the conversation a genuine "Me, too." Every time, the grandmothers would do an emotional double-take. They still were not accustomed to seeing their minister on his knees, literally or figuratively. But they did readily recognize that, yes, Tom did know and feel what they were talking about. The one who seemed at the center of things did understand exactly how it was to feel at the margins and forsaken. The one who could have been stalwartly aloof was humbled even as they. If there is redemptive effect to a great high priest sharing our common lot in suffering, Tom

Goddard showed how this could be. The one who had every right to stand in judgment on the grandmothers and whom they expected to scold and change them, to act like a good shepherd, beckoning them back to high ground, humbled himself and joined them in the thickets. The one whom they feared, or might have feared, fathered them in trust. The one who could condemn their feelings shared them. They were not isolated but joined, not reproved but matched. In Tom's ministry of "Me, too" they could relax their bristling defensiveness, admit their weakness and yearning, and open themselves to being found and to taking new steps in new directions.

They could afford to take a second look at the working mothers, to perceive their plight and not just their failures as partners. They could relax and accept the diversity of lifestyles; they could reaccept their own, even as they could recognize there was now also room for others'. At the same time, they were willing to look more deeply at their envy and resentment of the freedoms the younger women had. They could speak more openly and sharingly about these disquieting feelings, for each disclosure was met with another "Me, too." They could identify some patterns they genuinely envied and sometimes even began to imitate—more colorful and freer clothing, less compulsiveness about punctuality, more colloquial language with the children. They could sort out these patterns they envied and sometimes imitated from those against which they genuinely preferred their own styles, their family living patterns, for example. The grandmothers could take a more thorough look at their misgivings about their relations with the children, deepen the misgivings in some respects—the kids simply *were* unresponsive to their orderly directions—but also deepen the assurances in other respects —the kids did wink affectionately and even make moves to include the grandmothers in their play. The working mothers, who had seemed so intimidatingly strong, so self-contained, even self-centered, could suddenly be perceived as the fearful, marginal, guarded, intimidated people they felt themselves to be.

For Tom also ventured to add to his ministry of "Me, too" the ministry of "Them, too." It was far less dramatic for Tom to speak for the working mothers than for himself. But it still made the grandmothers do another double-take, open their horizons and share their lostness, as Tom led them to discover how similar their experience was to that of the working mothers. Tom, grandmothers, and working mothers all felt marginal and alienated, frustrated by broken promises, fearful of slipping competence and eroding identity. Tom did this in the context of a weekly Bible study group he had set up with the grandmothers.

Routines Re-deemed as Ministry

Tom's discovery of the power of the gracious words "Me, too" and his discovery that ministry was in abandoning shepherding more than in shepherding the abandoned changed everything even as they changed nothing. He still did Bible study; he still, as we shall see next, organized groups of people; he still preached. But he did all of these things in new ways, in a new spirit of sharing—in the communal bond of fellow lost sheep—in the spirit of the incarnation and cross, in the reenactment of God's redemptive, generous full intrusion into the human experience, of God's prodigal donning of the human plight. When living out this spirit yielded, before his very eyes, a new spirit in the life of the people, a compassion and an outreach, a binding and an opening, then he experienced the power of the gospel, quite literally and immediately, in a way he had never known before. The way of the fellow lost sheep was a more powerful way than the way of the good shepherd. The routines that had seemed tedious were re-deemed, in Tom's mind and experience, as ministry.

So Tom continued his weekly Bible study with the grand-mothers. But now what he said, and even more important, the way he said it, was faithful to the healing "Me, too" bond he had established with these women, as he expanded this bond to include "Them, too." He did not pretend that he knew less than they or less than he did about the Bible. But neither did he pretend that his knowledge was what the grandmothers needed to hear in the Bible or even that he knew what they needed. As it turned out, his own struggles and discoveries about the parable of the lost sheep helped him to share the struggles and discoveries of the grandmothers. He read the parable and asked the grandmothers "What does that parable say to us today? Who do you think are the lost sheep?" At first, they dutifully pointed beyond themselves to the "younger generation"; to the lower class and working groups; to non-Christians, non-Americans, nonwhites, or the unchurched; to the sick (said by those who felt healthy); to the widowed or those without families (said by those securely supported in tight families). (Later, when he would ask the same question in his Bible study with the working mothers, he got corre-sponding answers. For them, the lost sheep were also those beyond them, the politicians, the bosses, men, the younger generation.)

But, feeling the openness and the caring that Tom repre-sented, the women—some of them, and gradually—began to offer themselves, and each other, as among the lost. First it was said belligerently: "Why don't some of us admit that we, too, are lost?" Then more openly and fully: "Well, I do have times of not being sure where I am going and not knowing whether anybody cares." In Tom's newly discovered spirit of "Me, too" ministry, lost no longer was a mild invective (like sick or lazy or unfair or sinful) with which to fend off threatening people but rather a term of recognition and acceptance and hope.

Once they began to find themselves lost together, they began to find themselves. Exposed and shared, their misgivings about themselves and others began to be pared down and began to seek out answers. More and more, they began to seek out others, including the working mothers. So one conventional form of ministry, Bible study, unconventionally pursued, energized another conventional form of ministry, a women's organization, also unconventionally pursued because more in the spirit of lost sheep wanting to huddle than in the spirit of coercing or enticing—shepherding—others into the fold.

Tom had long known that it was part of his ministry that people should get together. The community is an important resource and an important expression of the church. So Tom, like most ministers, had tried to get people together. He had called meetings and organized groups and tried to marshall enthusiasm and impose community on the people. He was as skillful a good shepherd as any minister. The groups sometimes caught on and developed a life of their own, but more often they stayed hollow and withered. Imposed in this way by the minister, or by people on each other, togetherness becomes too much an end in itself rather than a resource for anything or an expression of anything.

It had always been part of Tom's daydream about the day-care center that, as the working mothers and children were brought into the orbit of the church, they would find ways to relate more intimately with others in the church; he had imagined something like a parent-teachers organization. But the daydream—instant community among diverse groups—made Tom cringe and groan too, for he recognized the extraordinary effort that would fall on him to build and sustain such a group, constant organizing and reminding and motivating and enabling.

Suddenly, in the new mood of "Me, too" ministry, all that

was different. He was taken by surprise one day to discover that the grandmothers and the working mothers had planned to assemble one Friday afternoon for a kind of party. Having begun to feel "Me, too" about each other, largely with Tom's help, feeling the bond of shared plight and common lot, they had begun to open up to each other more and more at the beginning and end of each day. Suddenly, they wanted to be together. *They wanted to be together.* Tom marveled at each word.

Tom had struggled so long throughout his ministry to make it happen that way. As a good shepherd he had used all his skills and talents and persuasion to get *them* to *want* to *be* together. But it had never really happened. His shepherd's crook to herd the sheep—his skills and talents and persuasion —had been as debilitating as it had been enabling. It had kept people focused on him and away from each other; it had kept people resisting the crook and the herding; it had kept people from exploring and testing what *they* wanted and could do. "Imposed community" is a contradiction in terms; but how else to achieve community, or any other goal of ministry, then by managing to become an imposing minister? In his new style Tom was not abdicating ministry and leaving people on their own. Quite the opposite: He was entering into the people's lives and into ministry in a far more effective, though far less obtrusive, way. He was only abandoning his crook and his herding role. He was abandoning, with a wrench, to be sure, the most visible and most popular signs of ministry. After the women began meeting in genuine community, no one (not even Tom) thought to say that he had got them together. They wanted to be together. He had not made them get together. He had done that which made them *want* to be together and able to *be* together.

At the day-care center hair never did get combed much better, and tardiness was still common. But the grandmothers and working mothers were now very much in a collaborative enterprise where these things didn't matter very much. They lingered and talked to each other and brought each other to their homes, but this physical intimacy was not nearly so important as the spiritual intimacy that developed. When they looked at each other, even when wordlessly transferring children, they felt a bond and not a barrier. But the bond had been discovered by looking within the barriers as they were deeply and painfully felt.

Tom gave up a lot when he found his ministry transformed. He really did believe everything he preached in the first sermon on the parable of the lost sheep. He did feel required to be a good shepherd, strong, committed, effective, giving the kind of help that people needed. All ministers are so called and want to respond; it is the very power of that call and the vigor of our commitment to respond to it that besets us. We want to respond but find we can't; we lack the wisdom or the strength or the circumstances. Our call is frustrated, and with it our sense of our strength and our competence and our commitment. In our frustration everything in us wants to cling to that call, to reaffirm our strength, to reclaim and recall others to their role in our call as objects or as partners in our helping. We often need others to be these lost sheep, and want to insist that they be so, so that we can remain the strong, wise good shepherd. It takes special grace to admit one's lostness and to heed the new leading, new call, new roles, especially when one's good intentions are thwarted, especially when the call on which one has lodged so much identity is blocked. This is the grace that Tom Goddard felt that enabled him to look so squarely into the frustration as his day-care center project floundered. This is the grace that Tom managed to communicate to the grandmothers that enabled them to experience their lostness enough to feel found again.

It is also the grace that Tom shared with many others, be-

yond his intent or foreseeing, as he preached the second sermon on the parable of the lost sheep, just after he rediscovered with so much pain and clarity that, whoever else is lost,
we are. He had himself and the grandmothers in mind as he
preached. But it turned out that he spoke of the life of many
who felt alone and forsaken in their loss and grief—until they
heard Tom joining them in his sermon. For weeks after that
sermon people began letting Tom know that he had touched
them deeply. Parents with children removed or remote,
women with strange or estranging husbands, women and men
with jobs ebbing even in the shreds of satisfaction they once
possessed—these and many others signaled that they had been
reached with a healing word, the word to let go of the strength,
the need to do things for others, on which they clung; the word
to let go into their experience of lostness that they might be
found and find anew; the word to empty themselves that they
might be filled anew.

7. Ministry: In Place, No Place

As the time approached when he was to be taken up to heaven, he set his face resolutely towards Jerusalem, and sent messengers ahead. They set out and went into a Samaritan village to make arrangements for him; but the villagers would not have him because he was making for Jerusalem. When the disciples James and John saw this they said, "Lord may we call down fire from heaven to burn them up?" But he turned and rebuked them, and they went on to another village.

As they were going along the road a man said to him, "I will follow you wherever you go." Jesus answered, "Foxes have their holes, the birds their roosts; but the Son of Man has nowhere to lay his head." To another he said, "Follow me," but the man replied, "Let me go and bury my father first." Jesus said, "Leave the dead to bury their dead; you must go and announce the kingdom of God."

Yet another said, "I will follow you sir; but let me first say goodbye to my people at home." To him Jesus said, "No one who sets his hand to the plow and then keeps looking back is fit for the kingdom of God."

After this the Lord appointed a further seventy-two and sent them on ahead in pairs to every town and place he was going to visit himself. He said to them: ". . . carry no purse or pack, and travel barefoot. Exchange no greetings on the road. When you go into a house, let your first words be, 'Peace to this house.' If there is a man of peace there, your peace will rest upon him; if not, it will return and rest upon you. Stay in that one house, sharing their food and drink; for the worker earns his pay. Do not move from house to house. When you come into a town and they make you welcome, eat the food provided for you; heal the sick there, and say 'The kingdom of God has come close to you.' When you enter a town and they do not make you welcome, go out into its streets and say, 'The very dust of your town that clings to our feet we wipe off to your shame. Only take note of this: The kingdom of God has come close.' "

Luke 9:51–10:11

Ministry in Place: Rooted and Routed

Christian ministry must be in a place. The passage of scripture above, which testifies so dramatically to the radical place-lessness of Jesus' ministry and of those who would follow him, testifies equally dramatically to the placedness of ministry. Jesus' ministers must leave home and duties and possessions; they may or may not find lodging. But ministry must be lodged, fixed. This passage speaks of Jesus setting his face resolutely toward a place and of his intention to lodge in particular places along the way. God's intention to save the race finds only localized expression, in visits to particular dusty villages. When those on mission find lodging in a house, they are to stay in that house, however mean and confining it may seem, however much more grand and compelling the mission may seem.

To be sure, Jesus' ministry and all ministry in his name must ultimately break out of the structures—and break the structures themselves—in which we contain our lives, for the structures that house and shelter *do* confine and distort. But first, minister and ministry must inhabit those structures, as genuinely and as radically as God has inhabited human history; for the breaking, to be truly liberating, must come from within; blasting of structures from without tends to destroy the inhabitants along with the structures. The cost, of course—as unacceptable as it is necessary—is that ministry that truly lodges in structures consigns itself to suffer their fate and to become broken too.

To become located and lodged in a particular fragment of

human history, with a particular people, is the only way, God knows, to enter history redemptively. That is as true for a minister today becoming fully invested in a particular denomination, a particular parish, a particular household, a particular program within that parish, a particular conversation with a particular person—obscure and remote and mean as that parish may be—as it is for God becoming fully incarnate among particular people in a particular locality, as obscure and remote and mean as that setting may have been. But also, to become located and lodged in a particular fragment of human history, God knows, is to suffer the constrictions and rupture and grief that are the inevitable consequence of the localization and fragmentation. This is as true for a minister today suffering the grief over the failure or the constrictions of a parish program in which he or she has made a full investment as it is for God absorbing the pain and brokenness of a pained and broken people.

In the midst of the dramatic warnings of the nomadic placelessness and rootlessness of his ministry, Jesus just as dramatically uses a remarkable metaphor of fixedness and focus; the plowman. The fisherman or even the sower are more romantic and therefore more appealing metaphors. They cast nets or seeds, widely, uncertainly, yet hopefully. They expect many empty nets and unsprouted seeds, yet occasional and eventual rich harvests. Venturing wide areas of sea and of turf, and taking a long view of time while they patiently await a high yield, surely fishermen and sowers are metaphors more suited to the ministry of the itinerant Son of Man who has no place to lay his head. And elsewhere Jesus does use these metaphors. But just here, while emphasizing placelessness, he also invites his followers to be like the plowman, head down, not looking about, making a narrow rut and being careful to stay in it. Ministry, even the ministry that breaks itself open to new life, even the ministry of those ministers who must recognize themselves as nomadic pilgrims, especially such ministry, must be in a place.

Ministers are "placed" in their positions by bishops and synod presidents and by placement services of churches and theological schools. But the more crucial placement is done by the people themselves, as they signal to the minister just what place a "minister" has in their lives: the moral exemplar, the surrogate holy one, the good mother or father, maybe the pied piper whom the children all like and obey, the healer of marital discord, the salver of all conflict, the answerer of unanswerable questions, the asker of embarrassing questions, the presider over a social status institution, the fragile link with a God once believed in or yearned for, the reminder of a simpler and purer lifestyle once enjoyed or yearned for, the surrogate believer or Bible reader or prayer or good neighbor to those in need— there is an endless number of places a minister occupies in the lives of people. For each person the place is different. For each person the place is usually well established and more or less clearly signaled. Such placement is seldom what the minister would choose.

Early New England churches would ordain a minister only to a particular parish; when the ministry in that parish ended, so did the ordination. The minister was no longer "reverend" until another particular people decided to call him so. Practically speaking, and any high theological convictions about the indelibility of ordination notwithstanding, this is still true. In a new parish a minister still must discover what it means to be "minister" in that place. Even more important, each individual "ordains" a minister every time the person says or thinks "reverend," every time the person tells the minister: Speak in a loud voice as though you had authority. Baptize my baby, and I will come back again when I have my next baby. Bury my father, as you did my grandfather. Come visit our home or our club and bless our food, but don't stay too long. Explain to the deacons where to stand while they are serving communion. Tell my boy to get off drugs. Can you find me a job? What are some good things to see if we visit Israel? Can you fix the mail slot on the church door? Be a man, but not *too* masculine; have an attractive wife who is not too sexy; have well-behaved children who are also well rounded. The daily ordaining calls are meaner and much less welcome than the ordination rhetoric that the minister would prefer. The abodes that Jesus' emissary is welcomed to are far less grand than expected by one sent out to proclaim the kingdom. Yet they are the real places where people live and where they invite the minister to inhabit. If the minister is to find a place in their lives, it must be, at least initially, in the place thus reserved. If the minister tries to carve or claim a different place, to say, "I belong in your life here not there," then the people are as amazed and perturbed as the householder who finds the guest choosing or imagining quarters different from those especially reserved. Then the people say no.

When Jesus entered *his* city, Jerusalem, he found himself welcomed to a place in the people's lives—that of the conquering Messiah, proclaimed with hosannahs—for which he knew he was misfit. But he occupied that place, playing the role to the hilt, living out their myths and expectations, because he needed to reach them to occupy their lives as they were lived. To decline the place reserved for him would be to act as though he were unwelcome altogether. The shaking of the dust is not for those who offer a mean or unfit place but only for those who offer no place at all.

When ministers are placed, they often feel *mis*placed. When ministers find a place reserved just for them—for *ministers*—in the lives of people, it is not always—in fact, it seldom is—the kind of place they would choose for themselves. Ministers would prefer other quarters than those they are shown to. (Indeed, after they lodge long enough with the people, they almost always *are* offered a different place in their household, usually a place different from that the people first designated and different from that the minister would first have asked for.)

Ministers would usually prefer a place closer to the family's intimate life and less "guest"-like. Ministers may prefer hospitality that is more informal, or else more formal, than what they are offered.

When ministers feel misplaced, they often confuse this with feeling unwelcome. When people offer them a place, even insist on a place of their own choosing, ministers may experience this as denying their own preferences (which may be spoken or unspoken, heard or unheard) and hence as a way of saying no to the ministers personally. Ministers feel unwelcome and like shaking the dust off with vigor and vehemence.

Exactly the opposite is true. What the minister experiences as misplacement is the strongest possible evidence of hearty welcome, even desperate welcome. The minister is welcomed into the people's lives in a place of their choosing, because that is important to them. The more they insist on showing the minister effusively to the quarters reserved just for "minister," and the more they are deaf to the minister's hints that different lodgings would be preferable, the more certain the minister can be that he or she *is* welcome, is wanted, is needed, really does have a place, a crucial and otherwise empty place, precisely in these reserved quarters. Precisely their deafness to the minister's hints for different lodging is what should make the minister want to listen all the more keenly to the hints as to why *this* lodging is so important for the people. Why do they need a biblical authority, or a question answerer, or a problem solver, so badly that they cannot hear the minister's clear hints of discomfort about being lodged in such places?

Coming into people's lives as a minister is like coming on stage in the late act of a long play, filling a part that has been well established in earlier acts, by different actors, and after a lot of dramatic action that has enmeshed that part with the roles of others. No minister starts fresh to create the role to his or her liking (or to the liking of professors or others who have coached the minister in how to play the role). The role is well established in its relations with others. The drama has gone on long enough to structure the plot securely, so that whatever part the minister has now *is* essential in the economy of the drama. To be sure, the drama is not finished, and the new minister will begin to reshape the story. But the reshaping does not begin afresh; it begins where the drama now is. The minister can begin to learn from the reactions of others just what this role is and maybe even begin to infer its history.

That this minister is not treated as he or she wants to be treated but is treated as the people want—that is the strongest possible evidence of an important and welcome place in their lives.

To be a minister is sometimes like overhearing one side of a telephone conversation but not realizing it is a conversation with a third party. Suppose you are in one room and you hear a person in another room speaking. The words sound strange, a bit off focus, not really directed to you as you understand yourself. "I wish you wouldn't play your records so loud," you might hear, when you don't even play records at all. You start to defend yourself, to straighten out the speaker, to explain how wrong he is about you. Then you walk into the speaker's room and discover that he is not talking to you at all; he is on the telephone. Suddenly you can drop your defensiveness, empathize with the speaker, join him in his complaint against the loud records. Being a minister is very much like that—with the special complication that people are often looking right at you instead of talking into the telephone. But what is happening is exactly the same: People only *seem* to be talking to you when, in fact, they are dealing with somebody else and they need your help to do that. Even though you are in the room where you know you belong, when they place you, they are really talking on the telephone to somebody else and they need you by their side, in their room, while they do that. To be a minister is to give up your preferred place and to be willing to be misplaced, in order to be in the people's place; then to experience the no-place—or perhaps the new place— of standing by.

Leaving Place to Find Place

"Let your bearing towards one another arise out of your life in Christ Jesus. For the divine nature was his from the first; yet he did not think to snatch at equality with God, but made himself nothing" (Phil. 2:5–7).

To be a minister is to know the theological (and maybe even the sociological and psychological) significance of baptism— and to be right about that and able to communicate it meaningfully—yet still to be willing, for the time being, to give all that up and to accept the misplacement of being called in merely and casually to baptize the new baby. Such misplacement is accepted in order to have *a* place in the life of the parents, the only place they have available for a minister now. Maybe it's like having to be born in a stable because there is no room in the inn, or even like riding a donkey and fitting into people's hosannahed expectations of messiah even when you know better. Once in place though misplaced, then ministry proceeds in the new place, which feels like no place, which is located, and momentarily bounded by, the parents' urgent need to have the baby baptized. Ministry is to stand by in that place, in their place, and give them room to discover more fully whatever yearnings and fears are lodged in their earnest questions, and also to discover whatever responses these yearnings and fears are pointing to. Ministry is to accept the misplacement so as to open it up, address it, and come to find it replaced. The parents' misplacing concerns may be several: awareness that their parents, who expect baptism and many other things, are looking over their shoulders; some sense of presumption and loneliness in daring to have a child and make

claims of adulthood; some "Is that all there is?" letdown am-
bivalently mixed with the joys and hopes of child rearing; some
dim sense (more and more likely these days from ecological
consciousness than from any explicit Christian theology) that
any new life is to be held in precious stewardship and to be
shared, as a hedge against squandering.

It sometimes happens that parents, exploring these misplacing concerns with sufficient freedom and space, come to address them with just those theological ideas the minister could
have announced in the first place. It also sometimes happens
that both parents and minister come to new places, the minister replacing his or her initial ideas, too, or at least discovering
that they find new focus as they find locus. Ministry that de-
clines the proffered placement as unsuitable seldom finds
lodging or effect.

Ministry is *in* all of the displacing demands and denials—just
say the table grace at our club dinner, don't speak of homosexuals, live the closely inspected exemplary life, accept the ten
percent discounts and other demeaning courtesies—without
ever being defined by them. They locate ministry but do not
identify it. They indicate *where* a minister can respond but not
how.

Accommodations Resisted

Ministers wrestle with their calls, even as did those whom
Jesus commissioned; they must decide whether to lodge or to
move on. There are more formal and public calls: the call to
ministry—whether to lodge in one particular vocation or another—and the call to a parish—whether to lodge in one particular location or another. When these public calls are at
stake, the minister is expected to and accustomed to struggle,
to try to discover whether the welcome (and needs and possibilities) of that "village" outweigh its limitations, chiefly the
limitation that it is only *a* village, one of many. Ministers rec-

ognize that they must give up some of their own preconceived or preferred expectations as to ideal vocation or ideal location, and also abandon, or learn to live with, misgivings about the proffered call. Jesus told his followers to test out the village. Ministers know how to test out the village when they are dealing with these more formal and public calls.

The informal daily, even hourly, calls that are lodged in particular conversations with particular people are just as crucial, just as fraught with the same questions, just as much in need of struggle and testing; yet it is not expected or even accepted that ministers should respond to these calls with the same testing, the same deliberate abandon of expectations, the same deliberate immersion into what is recognized as only a lodging—only *a* lodging, but a lodging nonetheless.

There are social realities that a minister must decide whether or not to live with and to work through when he or she is deciding whether or not to locate in the profession at all, in a particular denomination, in a particular parish. Analogously, there are social realities that a minister must decide whether to live with and to work through when deciding whether or not to locate in a particular role expectation of a particular person. When faced cleanly and openly, the social realities and limits of the profession, denomination, or parish usually can be accepted and worked with but carefully allowed not to exert sovereignty. Just because they are not faced openly and cleanly, the social realities and role expectations in the casual, informal calls are often allowed both to exert a sovereignty and to evoke bitter defiance. The suggestion here is simple: Face just as openly and deliberately and freely the limited and limiting role expectations in the daily demands and denials of more informal encounters between minister and person. Accept these calls, too, as occasions or locations for ministry, without fearing that they are sovereign blueprints for ministry.

A call to ministry is like a seed, about which Jesus talks so much. It is held carefully because it is precious and full of life not because it is fragile or weighted with threat. It needs to be planted, and that means it must find rooting in one place, one limited and specific piece of turf, not necessarily the most fertile. It also needs to break open. The seed will never be the same again as it emerges into the new and fuller life once locked within.

Typically, ministers resist accommodations vigorously. When the people say, "No, we won't accept you in the role and mission you have cast for yourself," ministers often respond as violently as the disciples ventured: "Lord may we call down fire from heaven to burn them up?" And when the people say, "You must . . . ," ministers often turn away and turn back as stubbornly as did those to whom Jesus said, "Follow. . . ." In the spirit of this book, this resistance, like any, invites exploration.

Ministers resist accommodation. This is partly because ministry needs to resist accommodation and confinement; ministry must constantly explode the niches into which people would cache it and their own lives. This is the proper ministry of the one who healed when not authorized, plucked grain when hungry, even on the Sabbath, disappointed the Palm Sunday fans, overturned the temple way of life, and constantly frustrated the disciples' presumption to be understanding Jesus and pinning him down. Ministry is in breaking out of accommodations, the ministry of one who has nowhere to lay his head. But these restraints can be erupted only from the inside, and one must willingly, even wholeheartedly, enter the prison (if that is what it feels like) before breaking out of it. Ministers tend to resist accommodation by shaking the dust off their feet prematurely, before they have walked down the dusty road into the village.

Why do ministers resist the lodging for ministry that is proffered in particular "calls?" Is it simply that ministers must safeguard the purity of their ministry and therefore, out of hand, separate and alienate themselves from the misplacing and displacing calls, the peculiar roles into which people would cast ministry? Perhaps ministers *are* sometimes the un-bending, unmoved sentries guarding the purity of their own call from the encroachment of daily calls. Perhaps ministers *are* sometimes that uncertain about the integrity of their call. But more often, I think, it is something else. It is not because ministers hold themselves aloof and remote by predisposition; it is quite the opposite.

Ministers tend to be those who are predisposed to get very easily involved in the lives of others, to be eager and willing to take up lodging wherever and whenever offered. They may frequently be guarding against too easily giving in to their own yearnings for intimacy, their own inclinations to belong, to join, to blend with the lives of others. It is not so often that ministers don't know how to settle comfortably into a prof-fered niche in another's abode; more often they know just how easy it is to do that, especially for themselves.

Further, I think ministers not only know how easy it is for them, almost so easy as to have to be guarded against. Ministers have much experience in past intimacies, in having let them-selves live fully into the accommodations offered by others. They have learned that such accommodations are never as permanent or as comfortable or as satisfying as they hope, and sometimes even allow themselves to expect. By theological conviction, but also by hard experience, ministers are aware of the risks of idolatry and other addictions. Ministers have come too close, in their own fantasies and in their own experiences, to yielding sovereignty to appealing invitations. They know what it is to yield to an attractive "Come on in, big boy." They know the disappointments that lie within, the promises unkept, the lonely abandonment. Ministers tend to be placeless people out of principle, and out of principle reinforced by hard experience. They know what it is to be well placed, firmly placed, or to want to be, and they know the grief that lies therein.

Look closely at the two excuses or explanations offered by those whom Jesus invited to join his journey. "Let me go and bury my father first. . . . Let me first say goodbye to my people at home. . . .": overcommitment to past bonds, and the grief that lies in their inevitable breaking, the grief the greater because the commitment was the greater. My past lodgings are important, and the ruptures are painful and need attention. I will follow, but there is grief in leaving the past. Ministers know this. And ministers know, too: I would follow a new call, even a meager and unpromising one, just because I am a determined follower, but I know the grief that lies ahead in that, too. If I get as committed, as invested as I know I will, it will hurt all the more when I finally get stranded, let down, as I know I will. "Let me bury first those longings for intimacy and readiness to find accommodation that have fathered my ministry." Let me do the grief work now in advance so that I can be freer to go out on the limb you point to. Let me have a garden of Gethsemane to comprehend and gentle the pain in every call before I follow it.

But Jesus' answer is just as stark as the one he discovered in his garden of Gethsemane: The grief cannot be avoided. It is part of the package, part of the ministry, and that is good. You cannot make full commitment unless you risk the certain grief that lies within it. Ministry of the ever-living God who so gloried in his creation that he could enter fully its groanings, and absorb fully its death—such a ministry is for one who longs more passionately than anyone for sure abode, yet is ever ready to find no place to lay his or her head. Such a ministry is for one who is so energetically ready to announce the new age, the new way, to anyone and everyone, that the grief and the risks known from hard past experience, though not blinked at, seem not so freighted with care as to make one withhold from new accommodations.